2020 Hindsight, Trump

A Lyrical Review

by

Robert M. Lebovitz

ISBN 978-0-9971209-9-8

PREFACE

When it comes to identifying the most singularly dominant personage of 2020, Donald J. Trump wins in a walk. The year started off with his impeachment trial. It ended with Joe Biden on the cusp of being officially declared — over much bitter but unsupportable dissent — his presidential successor. Sadly, the year also featured outlier climate disasters, social strife on a massive scale, political acrimony that revived and validated long dormant antagonisms, and, of course, the vicious COVID pandemic. While these misfortunes were for the most part beyond immediate control and lacked singular identifiable culprits, some were magnified by long-standing general neglect if not outright malfeasance. Overriding such distractions, Trump managed to keep his persona a focal point of the media and Internet. He thoroughly lived up to the court jester role, giving succor to some while amusing many.

In hindsight, it should come as no surprise that late evening comics' obsession with Trump did become tedious. How can you lampoon someone who is already eclipsing others' efforts at hyperbole and even outright fictions? A second bit of hindsight, elicited by his rage and demands following his failed reelection bid, is that he disdains the average American in addition to having no respect for our constitutional democracy. I mean, really, flaunting his golf prowess while millions wait for financial relief? For vaccines? This so validated prior exaggerations that one had to wonder to what America, in his rousing MAGA slogan, he'd been referring. Stripping away the veneer, his mode and methods have been more chilling than entertaining, more Grand Guignol than Sweeney Todd. Yet despite, or perhaps actually because of this Trump deserves caricature.

I have explored Donald J. Trump's mischaracterizations of leadership in several forms: fable, as in *NUTS*; musical drama, **** !TRUMP! ****; and satire, *The Mocking of the President*. He was even a lurking, nonspecifically anticipated presence in my freshman opus of 2013, *To Be*, which work, extensively rewritten, is currently in print as the *To Be, and Not To Be* trilogy. While consensus on the Left is uniform and sometimes brutally disrespectful, the fact remains that Trump is held in high regard by a very large fraction of this nation. I submit that this reflects more than partisanship. Firstly, it's the natural expression of evolved personal taste and therefore subject neither to debate nor critique. But secondly, and perhaps more significantly, Trump holds up a mirror to ourselves, vivifies predispositions otherwise tamed by social realities — instruction and circumstance being high among these. Thus, when we laugh at him we are in many respects laughing at ourselves, which may be a good thing. He flaunts natal traits socialization and education endeavor to suppress, aggressive tendencies that we look to maturity to temper: exclusionary self-interest; unabashed immediate gratification and impulse satisfaction; and a preference for fable more than fact. Extracting unwholesome benefit from the immunity conferred by his high office, Trump did and does, said and says what many would, had they equal opportunity. This blending of his distinctive personality with amorphous popular attitudes gives him a high order of resilient relevance.

Several factors need to be kept in mind as we go forward into 2021 and beyond. Foremost among these is this substantial popular support Trump enjoys. In addition there is the nationalist, far Right dogma that has inserted into the GOP, which many suspect is an anti-democratic corruption. Much like the Canadian-American Father Coughlin of the 1930's, he gave voice to Fascist xenophobia and prejudice, rationalized these to impart a form of opportunistic legitimacy. The positive response of such a large fraction of our citizens to the Trump administration, to his personal views of our proper focus and our place among nations, to his encouragement of recidivist policies paints an undeniably different portrait of our national will than we enjoyed since becoming "leader of the free world." Most worrisome is the weakening of our two-party system of governance, the diminishment of cooperative, loyal opposition and democratic compromise, which were critical for our overcoming past crises. Trump's significance will not vanish with his being out of office. Others have learned from his mistakes as well as his successes and are eager to take up his torch. To laugh him off is to de-emphasize the real threat democracy, as envisioned by our founding fathers, America faces. Nevertheless, I offer this satirical, lyrical review since Trump's past and present need expression so that we may anticipate our future. The essence of tragedy, should it come to that, is its reflective inevitability.

In practical terms, politics is dominated by individuals no smarter, insightful, nor farsighted than ourselves. Those most visible generally have no more native affinity for the inner workings of the craft than do plumbers for theirs. Like a plumber, they learned what worked and what didn't, what efforts were worthwhile and what were unproductive, where money was to be made and how to get it. It doesn't take a detailed analysis of current media to realize that we have a dearth of statesmen/women. Whatever their path to visibility, the majority of those in elective office are entertainers at heart, show-people who can please and convince a significant fraction of the populace of their utility, of their right to an "hour upon the stage." Donald J. Trump is paramount in that regard. Personal flaws have seldom, after all, been a reason to discount leadership. The actions taken and their relative success determine how a leader will be judged. In that respect, Trump has much to his credit. Many of his policies and directives seem to be what a significant fraction of the citizens prefer. And yes, there's the rub.

The cover photo chosen for this lyrical play is a metaphor for the social and political separation that has become a dominant feature of life in a time of COVID. Unwelcome but seemingly necessary isolation has intruded upon our private lives. In the public sphere, Right and Left political wings have become more than simply distinct. They have become irreconcilable, virtually irrational one to the other. This opens the door to domination via dogma, the tyranny of "... because I know what's right." We can anticipate that the COVID scourge will be overcome. Its gloom and necessitated sacrifice will pass. This may not be the case for the revitalized desire for authoritarianism, which prosperity, even though unevenly distributed, had kept suppressed. Whether that is a good or bad result is another, equally judgmental matter, as is whether or not Trump, like some secular anti-Christ, is intent upon bringing about the destruction of all that disfavors him. The pandemic has brought out the best in many but, unfortunately, it has brought out the worst in some. We are not done with it. Hardship, suffering, and death are sure to make 2021 another difficult year. That customs and institutions, upon which our prior concept of democracy depended, have been damaged is beyond reasonable doubt. The question is: Has our social fabric been made less resilient by recent events, or more?

The utility of exploring what the current year revealed of ourselves and of the people who would guide the course of this great nation goes beyond entertainment, which is the minimum I hope to have achieved. The only guidance I would offer is that the more extreme, the more frenetic the snippets of dialogue in this lyrical review, the more likely they are to be direct quotes. So take the characters at their word.

Dallas, Texas. December, 2020

In addition to:

*** *!TRUMP!* *** *In Three Acts* (2019)
A musical parody tracing the path of Donald J. Trump
to the Presidency, culminating with his impeachment,
and the companion to the present work,

prior fiction by the author includes:

To Be: A Novel (2013)
A dystopian view of a future wherein needs exceed
means.

*To Be, and Not To Be: The Rise of Misplaced Power
and What It May Foreshadow* (2016,2018)
A three volume ("What Was," "What Is," "What Will
Be") dramatization of plundered retirement accounts,
Internet-enabled superposition, and geronticide.

*We Never Do Wednesday's: Apart Together - A
Couple's Alzheimer's Journey* (2018)
A novel of acceptance.

NUTS! A Fable (2019)
A fantasy of the rationalized destruction of tradition,
based upon 21st century social/political trends.

AMERICA LOST (2020)
Stories of Troublesome Times
A collection of short stories that resonate with the
problems of aging and of a malleable past being used to
misdirect the future.

2020 HINDSIGHT, TRUMP

SETTING:

Primary action takes place in the White House and various governmental offices in Washington, D.C. Additional action at convention sites, newsrooms, etc.

TIME:

January through December of 2020.

PROLOGUE

OPEN WITH TIGHT SPOT HIGHLIGHTING UPPER BODY OF **MAN**, STANDING EXTREME UPPER STAGE RIGHT. HE WEARS A SOMBER SUITE AND HAS THE VERY WHITE FACE OF A PIERROT.

(MAN scans audience, smiles weakly.)

MAN

Hello and thank you for coming. Nice to see you again. As you may recall, in that prior production I was more casual and sported a beard. At the end I put on a clown nose, as a not so subtle dig at the circus our governance had become. My Uncle Sam hat was a nice touch I thought. I was tempted to

- 1 -

bring it this time but didn't. Times have
changed, have become more serious. Real
laughter doesn't come so easily in recent
days. This entire year, 2020, has been very
disheartening in many immediate, practical,
and thoroughly unphilosophical ways.

"Your job or your life..." Really? Was that
choice really necessary???

> (MAN strolls to mid stage center.)

Concluding that prior presentation with the
end of 2019 was appropriate. It made
dramatic sense since we were on the cusp of
one of those rare instances in political
theater — the impeachment trial of a
president, in this case Donald J. Trump. You
all know how that turned out. It didn't
change many opinions about him any more than
it seemed to change his status, but the
event itself and our getting there certainly
revealed a lot about us.

> (MAN drifts further downstage, to
> apron.)

Looking back, it seems that for years many
didn't pay much attention to what was going
on. We were content to focus on ourselves,
which is understandable. Those with partisan
agendas, those with really strong feelings,
took advantage of that, were able to take
charge while too many of us slept. But
confusion — deliberate or incidental — still
abounds and I (points to his face) will play
the ghost of that recent present. So pay
attention and stay awake as we cavort.
Whatever are your preferences as to leaders.
stay awake to ensure they are who you would
wish them to be. If you choose honestly and
in accordance with your own best interests,
as Adam Smith argued, everything should turn
out for the best. That's not a promise,

merely a hope. But do think. Don't just
react and let yourselves be manipulated.

GRADUAL BUILD OF INSTRUMENTAL INTRODUCTION
TO ACT THREE OF *TURANDOT* BY PUCCINI.

I have my biases, as you have yours. Still,
we can all derive something useful from what
we are about to present. Consider it fairly.
Drama, even humor, will often yield insight,
if one can survive them.

MAN
"TOO MANY HAVE SLEPT"

(Based upon Puccini's "Nessun Dorma," from
Turandot.)

> (MAN sings intently but calmly, the
> antithesis of a show-stopper.)

*Too many have slept. Too many have
slept.*

SPOT STAYS TIGHT ON MAN'S FACE AS HE MOVES,
FACE ALWAYS FULL OUT, TOWARD EXTREME STAGE
RIGHT.

*Even some of you, you here enjoying
this splendid hall,
Chose to push aside fear, to banish it
With the warm thoughts held in our
hearts as hope.*

*True, the future was hidden from us
all.
We could only guess at what would later
come.*

Yet, yet, we never can escape our true
futures.
But must make hope ring true,
Force hope and truth to be as one.

Our efforts here are for your eyes, and
for your ears,
Perhaps to make you laugh,
But they're meant to touch your mind.

<u>SPOT SLOWLY DIMS WITH ORCHESTRAL REPEAT.</u>

So, do not trust hope itself.
It only silences fear.
That's hope's pitiable flaw.
Speak out, be such that truth may win.
Truth must win. Truth shall win.

<u>MAN, STARTS TO RAISE ONE HAND, IS BRIEFLY
BRIGHTLY ILLUMINATED FULL LENGTH.</u>

<u>BLACKOUT.</u>

END OF PROLOGUE

ACT ONE

(TRUMP leans forward, cocks head at
an angle as he addresses MULVANEY.)

TRUMP
What the hell was she waiting for? Why did
she drag her feet on filing those goddamned
articles of impeachment?

MULVANEY
To make the process as painful as possible
and damage your presidency, Sir.

TRUMP
And damage my reelection campaign while
she's at it. That Pelosoi's a crazy lady.
Like a bad dog — once she sets her teeth,
she won't let go.

MULVANEY
Twenty twenty will be a good year, no matter
what kind of stunts she and Adam Schiff try.

TRUMP
Shifty Schiff.... Another one trying to
reverse the last election.... I hate that
I'm lumped in with Andrew Johnson, Dick
Nixon, and Bill Clinton. They did bad
things. I've done nothing wrong. It was a
perfect, perfect call.

MULVANEY
Nixon wasn't impeached, Sir. He —

TRUMP
Is that supposed to make me feel better?

MULVANEY
Just clarifying, Mister President.

VOICE ON INTERCOM
Senator McConnell and Representative McCarthy are here, Sir.

TRUMP
Send them in.

  (MULVANEY rises as **McCONNELL** and **McCARTHY** enter. TRUMP motions for the former to take MULVANEY's chair. McCARTHY stands adjacent to MULVANEY. McCONNELL starts to speak.)

TRUMP
(Waving hand) Yes, Yes, I know. (To McCarthy) Couldn't you have blocked it in the House?

MCCARTHY
Sorry, Mister President. Nancy Pelosi kept a tight rein on her troops. The numbers just weren't there.

TRUMP
(Addressing McConnell) Well, he had it right. Sixty three MILLION elected me and 230 are trying to force me out. (Shifting gaze back to McCarthy) That's not democracy. That's sedition. That's treason. It's Obama who should've been impeached, not me. You know that. Everyone knows that. He should never have been given the oath.

MCCONNELL
Kevin just didn't have the votes.

TRUMP

All because we lost the House.... We have to turn that around in November.

MCCONNELL

It'll be different in the Senate. I can assure you of that, Mister President. We have a lot of help there. Acquittal is a lock.

MCCONNELL
"WITH A LOT OF HELP FROM OUR FRIENDS"

There's no need to fear that we won't see you through.
This trial won't last out the week.
The Senate's my pet and I'll manage my crew,
And we'll get the acquittal you seek.

Yes, you'll get off with a lot of help from our friends.
Yes, you'll ride high with a lot of help from our friends.
Yes, they'll acquit with a lot of help from our friends.

TRUMP

How will I make sure those loyal stay lulled?

MCCONNELL

I'll keep unflattering docs from the floor.

TRUMP

What will you do if a witness is called?

MCCONNELL

I'll simply have Graham say, "Sorry, no more."

MCCONNELL, MCCARTHY, MULVANEY

Oh, you'll get off with a lot of help from your friends.
Oh, you'll ride high with a lot of help from your friends.
Oh, they'll acquit with a lot of help from your friends.

TRUMP

What if Schiff whines the trial's too slight?

MCCONNELL

It's for me to decide what is fair.

TRUMP

Schumer bawls what we're doing is not right.

MULVANEY

Too bad, we've the majority there.

MCCONNELL, MCCARTHY, MULVANEY

Oh, you'll get off with a lot of help from your friends.
Oh, you'll ride high with a lot of help from your friends.
Yes, they'll acquit with a lot of help from your friends.

MCCONNELL

*Romney's no worry, there's no way he'll
gain ground.
Though it's clear he's got that image
in his mind.
There is no way support for him'll come
around.
Like before, there's none there for him
to find.*

MCCONNELL, MCCARTHY, MULVANEY

*Oh, you'll get off with a lot of help
from your friends.
Oh, you'll ride high with a lot of help
from your friends.
Yes, they'll acquit with a lot of help
from your friends.*

TRUMP

Do we need some Democrats to sign on?

MCCARTHY

We just need our bloc to hold.

TRUMP

*And what if some cry that it is just a
con?*

MCCONNELL

*I'll instruct Graham he needs to stay
bold.*

MCCONNELL, MCCARTHY, MULVANEY

*Oh, you'll get off with a lot of help
from our friends.
Oh, you'll ride high with a lot of help
from our friends.*

Oh, they'll acquit with a lot of help
from our friends.
Yes, they must acquit, they must acquit
with the help from our friends,
With a lot of help from our friends.

MCCONNELL, MCCARTHY, MULVANEY, (WITH TRUMP)
Acquit with a lot of help from your(my)
friends.
Acquit with a lot of help from your(my)
friends.

TRUMP
Fine, that's all fine. (To McConnell) But
even better would be dismissal. A beautiful,
beautiful and quick dismissal. You only need
a majority for that.

MCCONNELL
Not a good idea, I would suggest, Sir. Too
many of our friends are afraid an immediate
dismissal would look bad.

TRUMP
It already looks bad. It's very, very bad.
Bad for the country more than for me. It's
terrible.

MCCONNELL
I'm afraid, Mister President, several are
listening to Romney and want to see it play
out. In the long run, that will be for the
best, to make it a clean refutation of all
the nonsense.

TRUMP
Yes, exactly. That's what I want. A clear
statement of no collusion, that it was a
perfect call. Only, that Romney! I don't
trust him. He's still bitter, a poor and

very bitter loser. Terrible way to act.
Almost like he's an anti-Republican.

MCCONNELL
I can assure you the trial in the Senate
will be brief and not help the Democrats in
any way.

TRUMP
I want to hurt them, Mitch. I want pay-back.
I think I should testify. I want them to
hear it directly from me.

MCCONNELL
Sir, I'd strongly advise against that. The
trial will be a formality. We don't want
Leftist optics.

TRUMP
They put up such a stack of lies. All of it,
a pack of lies and a hoax.

MCCARTHY AND MCCONNELL
Yes. Exactly.

MCCONNELL
They've brought it this far and Schiff will
have his say. But we'll have ours, and ours
will be final. They need 67 votes but
there's no way Schumer will get them. Not
even close. Schiff will parade his people
but —

TRUMP
The people love me, that's so obvious, so
clear. They're as disgusted by what's going
on as I am. An awful, clear-cut deep state
conspiracy to undo an election. It's been a
witch hunt, a hoax. The fake news people
have given crazy Nancy way too much coverage
of her lies. Sad, so sad what they're
putting the country through.

TRUMP
"LISTEN TO THAT PELOSI"

Listen to that Pelosi.
See her guile, hear her damn lies.
Riling up the deep state.
Damn her smile, damn her spies.

But my base, they love me more.
They will love me no matter what.
They count on hearing me saying,
"I'll make America great again."
I'll make America great again.

Yes my base, they love me more.
They will love me no matter what.
You can hear them always saying,
"He's made us great again."
I've made America great again.

To hell with that Pelosi.
To hell with her damn smile.
To hell with leftist deep state,
And to hell with Pelosi's guile.
It won't matter what Schiff will say.
He'll never tarnish my style.

Since my base, they'll love me more.
They will love me no matter what.
They count on hearing me saying,
"I'll make America great again."
I'll make America great again.

Yes my base, they love me more.
They will love me no matter what.

You can hear them always saying,
"He's made us great again."
I've made America great again.

MCCONNELL
Don't worry about that Pelosi.
Let her flaunt her pose and her smile.
Her leftist lies will not play,
Despite her gift for guile.
The Senate majority's firmly in line.
Not even Romney can change this trial.

Your base loves you all the more.
They will love you no matter what.
We'll smile to hear them saying,
"He's made us great again."
You've made America great again.

TRUMP (WITH MCCONNELL)
My(your) base loves me(you) all the
more.
They will love me(you) no matter what.
I(We) will smile to hear them saying,
"He's made us great again."
I've(You've) made America great again.
I've(You've) made America great again.

INSTRUMENTAL BEAT THROBS IN BACKGROUND:

Dah, Didi Dah, Didi Dah Di Dah Dah

TRUMP (WITH MCCONNELL)
Yes, my(your) base loves me(you) all
the more.
They will love me(you) no matter what.

I(We) will always hear them saying,
"He's made us great again."
I've(You've) made America great again.
I've(You've) made America great again.

MCCONNELL
We'll get through this, Mister President.
We'll get through this just fine and get on
with your program.

INSTRUMENTAL BEAT AND LIGHTS SLOWLY FADE.

BLACKOUT

LIGHTS UP WITH TRUMP ON DIAS OF NATIONAL
PRAYER BREAKFAST. WELL-DRESSED WOMEN, MEN
AND CHILDREN ARE ARRANGED IN PEWS. AT
PODIUM, WITH PASTOR ROBERT JEFFRESS AT HIS
SIDE, TRUMP HOLDS UP NEWSPAPER.

TRUMP
See? "Acquitted." Acquitted!!! That says it
all. No crime. No collusion. It was a
perfect call. Just lies from crooked people,
scum. Pelosi. Schiff. Horrible people.
Horrible. And Comey, who was a disaster by
the way, and his coconspirators Strzok and
Page! It was evil. It was corrupt. It was
dirty cops. The Democrats' collusion
illusion.

> (JEFFRESS moves closer to trump. They
> clasp hands.)

JEFFRESS
Yes, Mister President. A terrible time for
our country. A time of illusion when what we
need are clarity and truth, truth such as is
written here, (lays hand on bible), in
scripture, in the Holy Bible. (To TRUMP) The
country is blessed to have you as our
Leader. In you, He is coming! (To the

congregation) Donald J. Trump! The Lord had his detractors, too. As with Him, the hypocrites and defamers shall not win!

JEFFRESS (WITH CHOIR)
"FINE TO BE HARD RIGHT"

(Gospel-rock beat)

Oh Lord, each night I had those same bad dreams.
Made bereft of You, caught up in agnostic schemes.

Kept awake by the way it might could have been.
But now we know there'll be no change of scene.
Praise God, that door's been locked and we should discard the key.
Our heaven-sent leader is here to show us the Right way.

(Fine to be hard Right. Yes. Yes.)
Feels good to be hard Right myself.
(Ohhh, yes.)
(Proud and hard Right. Yes. Yes.)
I'm feeling that way myself.
(Ohhh, yes.)

Non-believers' falsehoods won't matter, no matter how hard they try.
They'll realize the truth when comes time for them to die.
I sense the Good Lord standing there, right there at your side.

*To give you strength and calm you while
they all lied.
Our President, when I think of Jesus, I
think of you.
Yes, I think of how you, too, are here
to see us through.*

*(Fine to be hard Right. Yes. Yes.)
Feels good to be hard Right myself.
(Ohhh, yes.)
(Proud and hard Right. Yes. Yes.)
I'm feeling that way myself.
(Ohhh, yes.)*

*Never lose heart, Mister President, for
we never will.
Our future's bright again due to your
firm will.
There's no going back to those heathen,
Godless days.
Together we'll convert even the most
vocal strays.
Love is our message; loving the Lord
and His might.
With that there's no stopping our proud
march to the Right.*

*(Fine to be hard Right. Yes. Yes.)
I'm feeling that way myself.
(Proud and hard Right. Yes. Yes.)
Feels good to be hard Right myself.
(Time to be hard Right. Yes. Yes.)
(Proud and hard Right. Yes. Yes.)
Feels good to be hard Right myself.*

(TRUMP embraces JEFFRESS.)

                    TRUMP
Yes. Yes. Heaven sent. And acquittal. Total
acquittal.

          (TRUMP waves as he steps down from
          the dais and joins MULVANEY to slowly
          exit.)

                    TRUMP
(Softly, to MULVANEY) Can you believe that?
Can you believe that people believe that
bullshit? It's almost as crazy as that
impeachment bullshit the Democrats served
up.... Well, that's all behind me now. No
president should have to put up with treason
like that. But you can't tell what those
deep state Leftists, those dishonest and
corrupt people will do next. They're stone-
cold crazy.

                    MULVANEY
Yes, Sir.

                    TRUMP
Time to make them pay. Like that Vindman.
You saw. Everybody saw. Wore all those
medals to impress. Everyone saw. He looked
more like that round-faced kid on the comics
pages. And Sondland. He lied, too. Crazy
Nancy lied. Little Adam Schitt lied.

                    MULVANEY
Yes, Sir.

                    TRUMP
And can you believe that Romney??? He voted
with them! Used religion as his crutch so he
could falsely justify doing wrong. He
shouldn't be in my party. He's not a
Republican. He's another Never Trumper and
should be run out.

MULVANEY

I'll point that out to Senator McConnell,
Sir. We'll take back the House in November
and work on that.

TRUMP

Good. But those two, Vindman and Sondland —
who lied, who testified about what never
happened — they work for me. I want them
out, now. Right now. Out! Vindman's brother,
too. Another snake in the grass. Get that to
Esper. He'll know what to do. I don't want
people like the Vindmans serving in any
capacity.

TRUMP
"I WANT, I WANT, I WANT"
(Heavily syncopated)
*I want, I want, I want people who will
not say no.
The perfect kind of person
Is one who's eager to play.
Yes, I want, I want, I want people who
will not say no.
What they think won't matter
As long as they repeat what I say.*

*The trial is done.
I'm feeling good how it turned out.
No guilt or collusion, no smoking gun,
I can get back now to doing what needs
to be done.*

*November's near
And I will win reelection.*

Burying socialism is our most important task.
Four more years is the very least to ask.

Pliant followers are the key,
Shadows whose thoughts are only of me.

I seek, I seek, I seek those with ambitions,
Those striving upwards
For power of their own.
Yes, I seek, I seek, I seek those with ambitions,
But content to bask in my light
And make sure my lacks are not known.

I want, I want, I want folks who will simply say, "Yes."
They can have their petty intrigues
As long as they abide me.
Yes, I want, I want, I want folks who will simply say, "Yes,"
And who'll argue that I'm right,
Even when the facts disagree.

Perfect time
To attack those hidden traitors,
Those who frown at the games I play,
Those who connive and sneakily try to block my way.

Fall brings chill,
And I'll make the Dems all feel it,

Get Congress under our control,
Give them decades of minority in the
cold.

Surround me with those who'll say yes.
I want no one around to second guess.

I need, I need, I need those who'll
pause their own minds,
Those content to be good soldiers,
Quick to obey my every word.
Yes, I need, I need, I need those
who'll pause their own minds,
Seek to please me like good puppies,
Like Pence, and project that I'm Lord.

I want, I want, I want everyone to love
me.
As leader I'll show them the way.
I know more than do they.
Sure, I want, I want, I want everyone
to love me,
To be glad that they're on my side
And hang on to everything I say.

I'll use, I'll use, I'll use those with
ambitions,
Those striving upwards
For power of their own.
I'll find, I'll find, I'll find those
who'll pause their own minds,
Those who are eager soldiers
Quick to fertilize the seeds I've sown.

LIGHTS SLOWLY DIM.

*I want, I want, I want everyone to love
me.
As leader I'll show them the way.
I know more than do they.
I want, I want, I want everyone to love
me.
As leader I'll show them the way.*

BLACKOUT.

AT LIGHTS UP, TRUMP WITH MULVANEY IN OVAL
OFFICE, THE LATTER STANDING NEAR DESK.

VOICE ON INTERCOM
Secretary Esper is on two, Sir.

(TRUMP holds up one finger at
MULVANEY without looking.)

TRUMP
Mark, that Vindman guy is no longer on the
NSC. He's out. Couldn't be trusted. What can
you do?... Well, then kill his career. Give
him some shit job to do.... Let me know.

(TRUMP hangs up and turns to
MULVANEY.)

VOICE ON INTERCOM
Attorney Barr to see you, Sir.

TRUMP
Send him in.

(TRUMP remains seated as **BILL BARR**
enters, motions for him to sit. BARR
nods stiffly at MULVANEY.)

TRUMP

I got rid of Vindman and Sondland, Bill. Two
bad, really bad apples. And I'll get to the
others. Now, about Roger. I want this
terrible, unfair persecution of him called
off.

BARR

Well, Sir, he was convicted months ago. It's
in the court's hands now, a matter of
sentencing.

TRUMP

Then get him off somehow. He's not guilty of
anything. Not a thing. You know that.
Everyone sees that.

BARR

I'm aware, Sir, but I can't state that. That
wouldn't be proper for me to say at this
point. It's up to the Judge and the case is
very strong.

TRUMP

How about probation? She was unfair to him,
very, very unfair from the start. Unfair the
entire way.

BARR

Probation is an option, yes, but only after
he's sentenced.

TRUMP

(To MULVANEY) Mick, I'll speak with Attorney
Barr privately now.

(MULVANEY leaves.)

TRUMP

We can't please everyone, Bill. I know that.
But there are two key things. One, fuck your
enemies hard and, two, take care of your
friends. Roger Stone has been a loyal
friend. How can we get him loose of this net

of lies that the House has thrown over him?
Your people at Justice are asking for nine
years!

BARR
Seven to nine, Sir.

TRUMP
Well, take that off the table! Okay, he was
convicted, but so what? Jail time is unfair,
very unfair to him. You're the Department of
Justice, not them. Change the ... take that
off the table, Bill. Jail time would be a
miscarriage of justice. Recommend probation,
so I don't have to get involved.

BARR
I don't think that would look good, Mister
President. I'll go over it carefully and
make some appropriate suggestions for
consideration as to sentencing, perhaps some
adjustment.

TRUMP
Be fair to him, Bill. He's been a big help.
Even if he went over the edge a small, small
bit, we shouldn't be harsh. He's a loyal, a
very good and loyal friend.

TRUMP
"IT'S BEEN TOO CRUEL"
Bill, Stone has been so loyal,
As an ally and a friend.

Now I you need to get him off,
Bring this nonsense to an end.
It's been too cruel, for a man who's
been true.

If Roger's made some missteps,
Went too far with his good work,

Then put aside the verdict.
Everyone sees that judge's a jerk.
She's being too cruel, to a man who's
true.

I don't want him put away.
As the Chief it should be ... what I
say.

Don't think it's just for him.
It's for all who work my plan.
Show that you're on the Right side.
Do everything you can.
Don't be cruel, to a man who's true.

I don't want him put away.
As the Chief it should be ... what I
say.

BARR
The verdict was from the jury.
The sentence will come from the judge.
I'd try to get probation,
But I don't think she would budge.
She'll be cruel, since he worked for
you.

TRUMP
Yes, face it, that Jackson's biased.
She had him guilty from the start.
Now we should make it our fight,
Show them all we have a heart.
Can't be cruel, to a man who's true.
I don't want him put away.
As the Chief it should be ... what I
say.

Can't be cruel, to a man who's true.
Can't be cruel, to a man who's true.

TRUMP (WITH BARR)
Let's face it (I agree), that Jackson's
biased.
She had him guilty from the start.
Now we should (Now I will) make it our
(your) fight.
Show them all we (you) have a heart.
Can't be cruel, to a man who's true.

I don't want him (He shouldn't be) put
away.
As the Chief it should be ... what I
(you) say.
I don't want him (He shouldn't be) put
away.
As the Chief it should be ... what I
(you) say.
Can't be cruel, to a man who's true.
Can't be cruel, to a man who's true.

TRUMP
Keep in mind what I've said about loyalty
and friendship, Bill.

BARR
Yes, Sir.

(BARR leaves.)

TRUMP
(Into intercom) Have Mick come in now.

(MULVANEY enters.)

                         MULVANEY
Yes, Sir?

                          TRUMP
Stay tight with Barr, Mick. When I get back
from this India trip I'll want to do
something for Stone.... What's your take on
that WHO announcement? They've said that
COVID is a worldwide pandemic now. (Shakes
head) They're such a bunch of clowns. If
they hadn't all along been working for China
this wouldn't have gotten so out of hand.

                         MULVANEY
Yes, Sir.

                          TRUMP
And I wish that Fauci would say one thing
then stick with it. He keeps changing. I
don't trust him. No one does. Do you think
he's another of the Never Trumpers? Another
snake in the grass?

                         MULVANEY
He's a career scientist, Sir. I doubt that
he's playing politics. But it's a fast
moving crisis. I'm sure he wants to stay on
the right side of it.

                          TRUMP
Well, find out what else he's been doing,
who he's talking to. If he's going to be a
problem, I want to know.

FADE TO TRUMP ALONE IN OVAL OFFICE, ON HIS
TELEPHONE, THE TV SCREEN IS ACTIVE WITH FOX
NEWS.

          (TRUMP turns his face from the
          screen, leans into the handset.)

                          TRUMP
(Annoyed) I just saw that damn Judge Jackson
has given Stone forty months, Bill. Forty

                         - 26 -

months! That's more than three years.... I
understand. Still, she's crazy. She's the
one who put Manafort in solitary
confinement, for Christ's sake. They didn't
do that even to Al Capone, and he killed
people.... Fine. But what about the trial
itself? It was rigged. That one juror was
obviously biased, too. An anti-Trump person,
totally anti-Trump like that crazy judge....
Roger did nothing wrong, Bill, absolutely
nothing wrong! It's a miscarriage of
justice. It's cruel and unusual punishment
for nothing. Nothing. You see that. Everyone
sees that. No one will be surprised at
leniency.... It's a very harsh, cruel
sentence.... Well, I'll have to do something
for him when I get back from meeting with
Modi. For Flynn. also. They're good, loyal
friends. That's what I respect most.

BLACKOUT.

THE FOLLOWING SEGMENTS (SEG 1-4) TAKE PLACE
SERIALLY OR (PREFERRED) ON A FOUR PART
(QUADRANT ROTATING) STAGE.

LIGHTS UP ON SEG 1: TRUMP MEETING WITH MODI
IN GUJARAT. FILM CLIPS SHOWN BEHIND, ON BACK
WALL. INSTRUMENTAL BOLLYWOOD MUSIC IS
MODULATED ACCORDING TO ACTION.

> (CLIP: TRUMP and MODI side by side,
> on balcony waving to crowd, with
> colorfully dressed standees behind.
> Above is the "Namaste TRUMP" banner
> between flags of US and India.)

TRUMP
Namaste! Namaste! And hello to India. (Looks
to Modi.) This is a great champion of India
and a man I am proud to call my true friend.
As the great religious teacher, (with
careful diction) Swami Vivekananda, once
said: "The moment I stand in reverence

- 27 -

before every human being and see God in him,
that moment I am free."

(Sounds of positive crowd reaction.)

MODI
The meaning of the name of this event,
"Namaste," is very deep. It means we pay
respect not only to the person but also to
the divinity inside him.

(Bollywood music swells.)

TRUMP AND MODI
India is a true friend and partner.... Time
to embrace our friends.

(They embrace.)

(CLIP: Angry crowds of Hindus
attacking Muslims in Delhi, police
officers throwing rocks at them and
waving on Hindu mobs. Music fades and
clip ends on static image of a
bloodied Muslim man.)

BLACKOUT. END SEG 1.

SEGMENT 2, DR. FAUCI BEING INTERVIEWED ON
VARIOUS OCCASIONS. EACH EXCHANGE IS FOLLOWED
BY A BRIEF BLACKOUT, SUBSEQUENT SMALL
POSITIONAL CHANGES, AND DIFFERENT
INTERVIEWER.

LIGHTS UP ON FAUCI SITTING BESIDE DESK OF
LATE NIGHT HOST.

(HOST leans in toward his desk.)

HOST
Well, then, Doctor Fauci, does Trump say
things about COVID with which you simply
disagree?

FAUCI

I don't disagree with the substance. But it's often expressed in a way that I would not, in a way that leads to confusion. One has to be clear, avoid misunderstandings about what the facts are. My job is to provide a consistent, clear, rational view of this disease.

HOST

That sounds like a polite way of saying Trump's wrong. Wouldn't it be better to simply point that out? You're the medical expert, one of the nation's leading experts on infectious disease, in fact.

FAUCI

When you're dealing with the White House, sometimes you have to say things one, two, three, four times, and then it happens. So I'm going to keep pushing.

BLACKOUT.

(Soft, percussive beat builds in background.)

Dah Dah Dah, Didi Dah Dah (repeat)

LIGHTS UP ON FAUCI AT DESK, SPEAKING TO INTERVIEWER (UNSEEN) VIA HIS LAPTOP.

INTERVIWER

The spread of COVID has been officially declared a pandemic, according to the World Health Organization in Geneva. The country needs to know what's really going on, what to expect. Are we getting that from Washington? President Trump insists on denying that we have a serious problem, even when you're right there next to him.

FAUCI

(Exasperated) Yes, it has to be taken more seriously. I know that. I'm trying my best. I cannot do the impossible. What would you have me do? I can't correct him in real time, can't jump in front of the microphone.

INTERVIEWER

You will never say "China virus," will you?

FAUCI

No.

BLACKOUT.

LIGHTS UP ON FAUCI, BEFORE MICROPHONE, ADDRESSING A CLUTCH OF REPORTERS.

FAUCI

Sure, I have a responsibility. I'm the expert. You make it sound easy, but it's not easy. Somebody writes a speech. Then he gets up and ad-libs. He goes his own way.

(Indistinct voices. Fauci lowers eyes and rubs forehead.)

FAUCI

I'm a scientist, an expert in infectious disease, not a politician. All I can do is give medical insight based on my experience. I work for the National Institutes of Health not the White House. But the President appoints the Director of the NIH, so ... I'll share this: What I have to say is based on what's happening in the real world, not the world of fantasy. If President Trump starts attacking me personally, that'll be the signal that he sees COVID as more of a problem for his image and for his reelection than for the people of the United States.

(Instrumental crescendo then fade.)

FAUCI

My job is clear.

FAUCI
"HE DOESN'T OWN ME"

He doesn't own me.
I am just another guy on his team,
But he doesn't own me.
Don't think I can't say what I mean.

Trump can't tell me what to do.
And he can't tell me what to say.
Sure, when there's an interview,
He loves having me on display.
Still ...

He doesn't own me,
He can't change what I have to say.
I am on his team,
But I won't play the game his way.

So, I advise him on what to say,
But I can't tell him what to do.
He's going to have his own way
And make it seem that it's all true.

Even when grim, I must rely on fact.
I rely on data, on what's shown to be
true.
They define how we should act.
Disaster comes when leaders lack a
clue.

He might tell me what I should do,
But he can't tell me what to say.

- 31 -

Yes, when there's an interview,
He loves having me on display.
But ...

He doesn't own me.
I'm just another guy on his team.
He doesn't own me.
Don't think I can't say what I mean.

So, I'll advise him on what to say.
Just don't expect that is what he'll
do.
His intent is having his own way
And to make it seem that it's all true.

Even when grim, I must rely on fact.
I rely on data, on what's shown to be
true.
They define how we should act.
There's danger in leaders having no
clue.

So, I'll advise him on what to say.
Just don't expect that's what he'll do.
(Fade) His intent is having his own way
And to make it seem that it's all true.
I'll advise him on what to say.
Just don't expect that's what he'll do.
His intent is having his own way
And to make it seem that it's all true.

(Instrumental background beat
returns, builds, then fades.)

<u>BLACKOUT. END SEG 2.</u>

LIGHTS UP ON SEGMENT 3: MID STAGE RIGHT -
ELDERLY WOMAN AND ELDERLY MAN IN LOUNGE
CHAIRS. THEY ARE CASUALLY DRESSED AND
LOOKING INTO THEIR CELL PHONES.

DOWNSTAGE LEFT - YOUNG MAN ONE AND YOUNG MAN
TWO STANDING, BOTH IN KHAKIS.

(YOUNG MEN are static as ELDERLY
COUPLE speak.)

ELDERLY MAN
Can you believe this? My God. Another big
drop today. It's down over ten thousand now!
That's thirty percent!

ELDERLY WOMAN
It'll recover. He said it would.

ELDERLY MAN
Sure, love. That's what he said last week.

ELDERLY WOMAN
And he was right. It did.

ELDERLY MAN
Are you crazy? It's down three times what it
was last week. All because of COVID.

(Angrily) *Pandemic!*

ELDERLY WOMAN
(Melancholy) *Pandemic?*

ELDERLY MAN AND WOMAN
Pandemic!? Pandemic?!

ELDERLY WOMAN
"PANDEMIC"
(Melancholic, weak voice) *I fear the
situation has gotten out of hand.
I wish I knew the reason why*

- 33 -

COVID's come from some far off land.
They say it's 'cause so many people
fly.
You understand?

ELDERLY MAN
Pandemic!

ELDERLY WOMAN
Pandemic?

ELDERLY MAN AND WOMAN
Pandemic!? Pandemic?!

ELDERLY MAN
Don't know all the details. We probably
never will.
What's crashing over us right now
Is an avalanche screaming down a hill.
They're trying everything to gain
control.
Have they the skill?

ELDERLY MAN AND WOMAN
Pandemic! We're exposed to a new kind
of threat.
Pandemic! And we haven't seen the worst
of it yet.
Pandemic! We've lost so many of our
elderly friends.
Pandemic! We have no idea when this
will come to an end.
Pandemic! What if we both were to fall
ill?
Pandemic! Who would take care? How
would we pay the bills?

ELDERLY MAN
What's sad is every stranger brings a new threat it seems.

ELDERLY WOMAN
Because of COVID; because of COVID.

ELDERLY MAN
We wake up in the dark, sweating from our bad dreams.

ELDERLY WOMAN
Because of COVID; because of COVID.

ELDERLY MAN
The market's cratered; we have to hope it will come back.

ELDERLY WOMAN
Because of COVID; because of COVID.

ELDERLY MAN
That's another worry that we'll just have to track.

ELDERLY WOMAN
Because of COVID; because of COVID,
Even friends and family must stay distant these days.

ELDERLY MAN
Because of COVID; because of COVID.

ELDERLY WOMAN
We've become alone in so many cruel ways.

ELDERLY MAN
Because of COVID; because of COVID.

ELDERLY WOMAN

I miss the grandkids, we kept for them
that spare room.
It's just not the same having our
visits on Zoom.

ELDERLY MAN

Because of COVID; because of COVID.

ELDERLY MAN AND WOMAN

Pandemic! We're suffering a new kind of
threat.
Pandemic! We haven't even seen the
worst of it yet.
Pandemic! We've lost so many of our
elderly friends.
Pandemic! We have no idea when this
will come to an end.
Pandemic! Every stranger is a new
threat it seems.
Pandemic! We wake up in the dark,
fighting bad dreams.
Pandemic! Even friends and family must
keep distant these days.
Pandemic! We've become alone in so many
cruel ways.
Pandemic! What we do won't change a
damn thing.
Pandemic! We'll have to see what the
next few months bring.

ELDERLY WOMAN

How will we live?

ELDERLY MAN

We'll just live.

ELDERLY WOMAN
What can we do?

ELDERLY MAN
Nothing.

ELDERLY WOMAN
So, we do nothing?

ELDERLY MAN
I can shoot the bastard.

ELDERLY WOMAN
Who?

ELDERLY MAN
Our broker.

(ELDERLY COUPLE become static as YOUNG MEN speak.)

YOUNG MAN ONE
How did you hear?

YOUNG MAN TWO
They broadcasted a text. Had UPS come in to box up my stuff and send it to me.

YOUNG MAN ONE
They didn't give you any notice?

YOUNG MAN TWO
Sure, I got notice. The header on the text, the bastard.... What about you?

YOUNG MAN ONE
We turned the last tables Sunday night. The End. Can't make money running at 25 per cent capacity, she said. No point. Every plate costs her. And no bar??? Shit!!!

YOUNG MAN TWO
So what can you do?

YOUNG MAN ONE

Same as you. Hope this is over before the
unemployment runs out.

YOUNG MAN ONE

(Energetic and crisp) *Pandemic!*

YOUNG MAN TWO

(As above) *Pandemic?*

YOUNG MAN ONE AND TWO

Pandemic! Pandemic!!

YOUNG MAN TWO

*I was let go today; not even man to
man.*
I wish I knew the real reason why.
*The text just said it was not their
plan.*
But no clients means no income for pay.
Seems like it's hit the fan.

YOUNG MAN ONE

Pandemic!

YOUNG MAN TWO

Pandemic!!

YOUNG MAN ONE AND TWO

Pandemic! Pandemic!!

YOUNG MAN ONE

*That's not good for us, that I've lost
my job, too.*
*But always mostly empty's no way to run
a café.*
*I thought they could find a way to just
make it through.*

But, now, restrictions are tight and seem here to stay.
Boxing take-out is all they can do.

YOUNG MAN ONE AND TWO
Pandemic! No difference that they call it "furlough."
Pandemic! Can't change jobs when there's no place to go.
Pandemic! They had to cut back, sure, that was too clear.
Pandemic! Things will get better but it might take a year.
Pandemic! Working from home might be okay for some.
Pandemic! But we have to be on site to get our jobs done.

YOUNG MAN ONE
They'll try take-out, but it's not the answer they sought.

YOUNG MAN TWO
Due to COVID; due to COVID.

YOUNG MAN ONE
I hope it's over before our employment runs out.

YOUNG MAN TWO
Due to COVID; due to COVID.

YOUNG MAN ONE.
The system's rotten, it's built to favor the rich.

YOUNG MAN TWO

Shown by COVID; shown by COVID.

YOUNG MAN ONE

*Pols say they'll help us, but it goes
to their son of a bitch.*

YOUNG MAN TWO

*Shown by COVID; shown by COVID.
Just had a UPS man come and box up my
stuff.*

YOUNG MAN ONE

Because of COVID. Because of COVID.

YOUNG MAN TWO

*Shown to not count for much was really
quite rough.*

YOUNG MAN ONE

Because of COVID. Because of COVID.

YOUNG MAN TWO

*It's no fun being shoved out into the
cold.*

YOUNG MAN ONE

Because of COVID. Because of COVID.

YOUNG MAN TWO

*Makes you feel like one bought and then
sold.*

YOUNG MAN ONE

Because of COVID! Because of COVID!

YOUNG MAN ONE AND TWO

Pandemic! No difference that they call it furlough.

Pandemic! Can't change jobs when there's no place to go.

Pandemic! They had to cut back, sure, that was too clear.

Pandemic! Things will get better but it might take a year.

Pandemic! Half-way measures aren't the answer they sought.

Pandemic! Hope it's over before our employment runs out.

Pandemic! The system's rotten, built to favor the rich.

Pandemic! Pols say they'll help us, but it goes to their son of a bitch.

Pandemic! What we do won't change a damn thing.

Pandemic! We'll have to see what the next few months bring.

ELDERLY AND YOUNG (QUARTET)

Pandemic! We're suffering through a new kind of threat.

Pandemic! And we haven't seen the worst of it yet.

Pandemic! We'll need to cut back, sure, that's all too clear.

Pandemic! Things will get better but it might take a year.

Pandemic! The system's rotten, built to favor the rich.

Pandemic! Pols say they'll help us, but it goes to their son of a bitch.
Pandemic! Our friends and family must keep distant these days.
Pandemic! We've become alone in so many cruel ways.

Pandemic! Yes, friends and family must keep distant these days.
Pandemic! We've become alone in so many cruel ways.

BLACKOUT. END SEG 3.

LIGHTS UP ON SEGMENT 4: NEWS READER SITTING AT DESK, FACING AUDIENCE AND WEARING A GRAY FACE MASK.

READER

The White House insists that wearing face masks is not necessary and may even increase the chance of infection.

(READER takes off mask.)

BRIEFLY DARK.

READER

The Center for Disease Control has declared the COVID-19 outbreak a national emergency. In accordance with their guidance, Americans should wear "non-medical cloth masks" whenever outside, to help slow the spread of COVID-19.

(READER puts on mask.)

BRIEFLY DARK.

READER

President Trump clarified today that the wearing of face masks is voluntary. He will not make it national policy. "I don't think I'm going to be doing it," he said then added, "I just don't see it."

(READER takes off mask.)

BRIEFLY DARK.

READER

(Quizzical look) The President stated today that, "This is a very contagious virus. It's incredible. But it's something that we have tremendous control over."

TRUMP

(Offstage, voice muffled, as if a tape recording) I intended to always play it down.

(READER hesitantly puts mask on.)

BRIEFLY DARK.

READER

"Just stay calm," the President has today advised. "It will go away. We want it to go away with very few deaths." The President indicated he has great confidence in our response to COVID-19. "I'd rate it a ten," he noted.

(READER takes off mask.)

TRUMP

(Offstage, as if from a press conference) The only thing we haven't done well is get good press.... Stay calm, it will go away.... I haven't heard about testing being a problem. We inherited a broken test — the whole thing was broken.

(READER picks up face mask gingerly,
then puts it down.)

READER (WITH OFFSTAGE CHORUS)
"TRUMP WANTS IT HIS OWN WAY"

Covering up
Doesn't seem a big deal to ask.
So why does Trump
Say it's such a silly thing to mask?

Everywhere else
That's made the right thing to do.
So why not here?
With COVID unbound, it's best for me
and you.

But Trump wants it his own way.
(To have it his own way.)
He wants to have that macho, final say.
Trump wants it his own way.
(To have it his own way.)

Extra care
Seems wise until this crisis is no
more.
Then we all could
Go back to the way we were before.

If he could,
Fauci would have masks on not just
some.
But how can he
When Trump pokes fun and says that it
is dumb?

Yes, Trump makes masks the controversy
of the day,
(To have it his own way.)
When actually it's infectious disease
that's in play.
Trump wants it his own way.
(To have it his own way.)

INSTRUMENTAL INSERTION

READER (WITH OFFSTAGE CHORUS)
Avoiding crowds,
That's another plan that makes good
sense.
To responders, yes,
But not to our President nor to Pence.

And staying home
Would blunt the infection's terrible
spread.
Yes, that does hurt,
But it's better than many ending up
dead.

But Trump must have it his own way,
(To have it his own way.)
Hold rallies so he can hear them shout
"hooray."
Trump must always have it his own way.
(To have it his own way.)

I shouldn't preach
Because my job is reporting the news.
Yet I'd err,
If I didn't state what's clearly true.

Mask and hand wash,
To ensure those you care for stay well.
When COVID ends
We will have quite a story to tell.

Yet, Trump's had to have it his own
way,
(To have it his own way.)
Telling all that the pandemic will just
fade away.
He must always have it his own way.
(To have it his own way.)

Yes, Trump wants it his own way.
(To have it his own way.)
He wants to have that macho, final say.
Trump wants it his own way.
(To have it his own way.)

(Repeat and fade into following:)

READER
The CDC reported today that the COVID-19
death total continues to rise. There seems
to be little indication that the threat is
ebbing. (READER stares out, sighs, then puts
on face mask.)

BLACKOUT. END OF SEG 4.

LIGHTS UP ON MAN. HE WEARS A BLACK SUIT. HIS
FACE IS STARKLY WHITE.

MAN
I know what you're thinking. But not
everything is black and white. (He looks
about.) I shouldn't make jokes, but it's my
nature. Or was, at least — COVID has taken a
bite out of humor. Anyway, COVID has hit

Europe hard. So, do you really think we're
going to avoid that here? Ha. Not without
good management and a lot of good luck.
Management and luck.

Italy has chosen to lock down and Sweden has
decided to let it rip. So, here's the
dilemma we face: Do we lock down and have
many lose their jobs? Or do we keep
everything open and accept that many will
lose their lives? Business versus public
health — that's going to be a hard pair to
reconcile.

MAN
"TO CLOSE OR NOT TO CLOSE"
(Poetically declamatory.)

*To close or not to close, that is the
question.*
*Whether it's better for business to
suffer*
The immediate pain of quarantine
*With the hope that the crisis will
pass,*
Or to let crowds gather
And let nature take it course,
*To let the infection spread and thus
more quickly quell*
The illness that has become a pandemic.
*Blunting transmission from one to
another,*
Herd immunity. Yes, it's a worthy goal.
We need it; we wish for it,
For then some but not as many will die.
Ahhh, there's the problem.
For to achieve that desire state
How many more must leave this earth
Must give us pause and have us reflect

Upon those who would not wish to be so
used,
Who have no wish to feel their lungs
fill with fluid
And suffer loss of the means to
breathe,
Except for what some machine may
provide.

>   (MAN paces side to side. He stops,
>   then resumes his recitation.)

To recover yet not be well?
To yet suffer months and years of
defect
Just so others can enjoy their freedoms
to act
And not be constrained by fiat?
Who would give up themselves for this?
Who would give up the ones they love,
So that the sickness would more quickly
pass from others
And make safe mere strangers
Who will not know their names?
Whose names they will not know?
Death is no reward for sacrifice.
It is the price that they will have
paid.
Is this truly a war, with an enemy's
face,
Where the sacrifice of one
To save another, to save the many, has
merit?

No, that is the fantasy that some would
impose,
That we must choose between pandemic
and depression,
That WE must choose between those who
will die
And those who will thrive.
How feeble, how hollow is that logic.
How poor, how base is the notion
That the success of enterprise
Conflicts with the health of a nation,
That we must take a side against the
many dying
Or against the many losing their
livelihoods.
Framed so, the paltry powers of
government
Make themselves evident
And those who lead
Have lost the validity of their
leadership.

MAN
(Slowly scanning audience, normal cadence.)
November seems a long way off. But it'll be
here before we know it. Whatever happens,
this administration is going to have a lot
to answer for. And the next, whether new or
simply a continuation, is going to have much
waiting to be addressed. Whoever wins, there
will be much to manage. They will need that
good luck!

(MAN moves offstage as lights dim.)

BLACKOUT.

- 49 -

LIGHTS UP ON OVAL OFFICE. TRUMP WITH MARK MEADOWS, HIS NEW CHIEF OF STAFF.

> (TRUMP nodding, watching Fox News on TV. MEADOWS, seated across desk, peers over his shoulder. TRUMP turns away from set, smiles.)

TRUMP
Well, Sleepy Joe has the Democrats in his pocket. He'll be their nominee.

MEADOWS
That's a good thing, Sir.

TRUMP
Yes. Everyone will realize he's not up to the job. He looks and acts old, an old loser half asleep.

MEADOWS
We've already got his weak points out there. You can keep hammering on them.

TRUMP
(As if not hearing) Obama made a big show of endorsing him. Like he just came down off some damn mountain. A big joke. A huge, huge joke. Everyone sees that's a joke. (Scoffs) Obama. He's the one who should have been impeached. Should never have been sworn in.... He's more African than American.

> (Instrumental jazz beat begins.)

TRUMP
Why does the Democratic party attract so many blockheads?

MEADOWS
Good question, Sir. It's the nature of their philosophy.

                         TRUMP
Blockheads. Good name for them, but I like
better what I coined for little Shifty
Schiff.

                        MEADOWS
You called him Watermelon Head, as I recall.

                         TRUMP
And the media loved it. The ignorant little
man earned it. I should stick that title on
Obama. Watermelon Head.

                        MEADOWS
I don't think that's a good idea, Sir. You
can think it, but can't say it. Some would
say it's racist.

                         TRUMP
Probably right. The fake media would jump
all over it; create a big deal about
nothing; call me a racist when I'm the least
racist person I know, the least racist in
the country. Blacks love me because I've
done so much for them. More than anyone. It
is sad, so sad, though, that Obama was such
a disaster, such a Watermelon Head.

             (TRUMP stares out, his facial
             expression reacting as MEADOWS
             sings.)

                        MEADOWS
                 "YOU'VE EXPOSED THAT MAN"
Oh, you've exposed that man.
Yes, Watermelon Head.

HEAVY ORCHESTRAL JAZZ BEAT.

  So true, he wasn't even born here.
  It's clear, his two terms were
  disaster.

                       - 51 -

*He spied on you, to see if he could
find dirt.
End of day, it was he himself who got
hurt.
He took an oath but, yes, you've
exposed that man.
Oh, you've exposed that man.
Yes, you've exposed that man.*

*You've said, Obama enabled ISIS.
Since him, all we've had is crisis.
So dumb, he let the Iranians bait him.
So bad, he made the generals hate him.
For the record, yes, you've exposed
that man.
Oh, you've exposed that man.
Yes, you've exposed that man.*

*And there's more that's certainly worth
the telling.
Can't believe what that Obama man was
selling!*

*Oh, you've exposed that man.
Yes, you've exposed that man.*

*Swine flu? The man did such a poor job.
Care act? A scam just to please his
Blue mob.
Sleepy Joe has taken up the same plan.
With Obama's baggage, you'll make him
sorry he ran.
Affordable care? Ha!*

You've exposed that man.
Oh, you've exposed that man.

Yes, Watermelon Head.
And there's more that is worth the
telling.
Can't believe what Obama was fond of
selling.
Had you run, you easily would have beat
him!
Yes, Watermelon Head.
Yes, you've exposed that man.
Yes, Watermelon Head.
Yes, you've exposed that man.

(TRUMP nods, continues to stare out.)

TRUMP
Absolutely. I had so much to use against
him. That Romney was such a pussy. It was
criminal that Obama lost to him. Criminal. I
would have won in a landslide.

MEADOWS
Absolutely, Mister President.

TRUMP
Obama's endorsement is going to be a big
negative for Sleepy Joe.

MEADOWS
Yes, Sir. There's a lot of resentment over
that affordable health care and guns and -

TRUMP
(Interrupting) Many of his own people don't
like him, I hear. Biden, I mean. The Sanders
people certainly don't.

                    MEADOWS
It's a fractured party.

                     TRUMP
And the Leftists are pushing them into a
corner, God bless 'em!!!

                    MEADOWS
They don't know what they want, what to
focus on.

                     TRUMP
I do, damnit. First, I want to get this
virus thing behind us. COVID. That's what
the fake media keeps harping on. COVID,
COVID, COVID. Once we get past this pandemic
hoax everything will fall into place.

                    MEADOWS
Yes, Sir. That and the economy are linked.
Both very important.

                     TRUMP
Very, very important. Key, Mark. Key. But
That Fauci fellow is making it difficult.
Every time I put a good idea out there —
like that hydroquinone — he makes a face or
claims it won't work. COVID, COVID, COVID.
Face masks, face masks, face masks. Always
with the face masks. That doesn't kill the
virus, does it?

                    MEADOWS
No, Sir.

                     TRUMP
And that's what we need. Bleach or
something, to kill the virus. At least until
a vaccine is ready. Good thing we got rid of
that Bright guy. He became another one of
those disgruntled employee. (Shakes head)
Glad to be rid of him. Awful, awful. He
never did a very good job. It's good he's
gone. There are some others who need to go,

also. Awful. We'll focus on Operation Warp
Speed. Get that on track and in the media.
Our guys at Fox will cover it. We need that
vaccine before the election.

MEADOWS

Yes, Sir.

TRUMP

Anything that might help is good. Even that
bright light idea, that ultraviolet. I've
been doing that for years. That's why I look
so good. Why I look so young and healthy.
Like a much younger man. I think that's why
I'll never get COVID. I don't need to worry
about it. No one does, really. It's just
another flu. We don't have to let it
dominate us.

TRUMP
"PROTECTED BY THE LIGHT"

Protected by the light.
No need to hide my face,
I can demonstrate our rights.
Protected by the light.
No need to hide my face,
I can demonstrate our rights.

We have that pill,
In case we suddenly should get ill,
That keeps us from getting real sick.
It's been proven that it works,
Despite those nay say jerks,
As long as you take it really quick.

Those at rallies needn't mask.
Although Fauci says to ask,
He's not one of those whom I trust.

I'd rather take my chances,
Because the clear and simple fact is
There's a difference between what we
should and what we must.

Yes, I'd rather take my chances,
Because the clear and simple fact is
There's a difference between what we
should and what we must.

MEADOWS
Protected by the light.
No need to hide your face,
You will demonstrate our rights.
Protected by the light.
No need to hide your face,
You will demonstrate our rights.

TRUMP
The Docs' put out a new plan,
Every time they think they can.
It'd be better if they spent time on
vaccines.
We can't have each day,
Come with something new for them to
say.
The true plan's what my White House
team means.

I don't care what they do abroad.
Here we'll take a better road.
The economy must not fall back.

Public health is a concern,
But so is what they earn.
We must ensure the economy stays on
track.

TRUMP (WITH MEADOWS)

Protected by the light.
No need to hide my (your) face,
I can (You will) demonstrate our
rights.
Protected by the light.
No need to hide my (your) face,
I can (You will) demonstrate our
rights.

TRUMP

People are always dying,
There is no use in crying
If they go from that or from this.
When an economy is in tatters,
There's little else that matters
When an income is the biggest thing
they miss.

The economy must stay open,
Not collapse while we're all hoping
A vaccine will bring COVID's end.
With so many relying,
On working and not on dying,
We must stay on plan till we're 'round
the bend.

I know we'll be safe
Our health saved by UV light.
No need to give in to MDs.
The public will recognize that I'm
right.

I've learned, never to back down from
those who think they know more.
I've learned, that money's the way to
keep score.

MEADOWS
Protected by the light.
No need to hide your face,
You will demonstrate our rights.
Protected by the light.
No need to hide your face,
You will demonstrate our rights.

TRUMP
Just 'cause they put on white coats,
Doesn't mean they get to steer our
boats.
There much to do besides spreading
fear.
It's confidence that we need,
Not some scary worst case screed.
It's best to promise a cure is quite
near.

We need that task force,
I've put Jared in charge, of course.
So without Dems, it will do more than
try.

I trust him like my own son.
Jared's the one to get it done.
He's almost as smart as am I.

Protected by the light,
No need to hide my face.
I will demonstrate our rights.
Protected by the light,
No need to hide my face.
I will demonstrate our rights.

TRUMP (WITH MEADOWS)
Protected by the light.
No need to hide my (your) face,
I (You) will demonstrate our rights.
Protected by the light.
No need to hide my (your) face,
I (You) will demonstrate our rights.

BLACKOUT.

END ACT ONE

ACT TWO

TRUMP
The CDC has become a big problem, Mark. It's as big a problem as the virus. Need to shake it up. Get some of our own people in there. That Messener isn't helping.

MEADOWS
(Carefully) Yes, Mister President. Doctor Messonnier could be more supportive.

TRUMP
Always so negative, so negative. Get her out of there. I don't think Redfield is helping either. Not helping me at all. It seems that the entire agency has gone rogue, is trying to make me look bad. We need to get them in line, provide closer oversight.

MEADOWS
Yes, Sir. They haven't been providing a useful long term view.

TRUMP
What we need is a real solution, something with good optics. Not all the "wear this, wipe down that, keep your distance" Leftist propaganda that's killing the economy. I don't think the Democrats want to see the pandemic end at all. Not until after November. They're using it to help them in

the election, saying to hell with the
economy and the people who get COVID, just
to win back a few more seats in the House.
That's sick. Very, very sick. I don't know,
it just seems that way. Maybe they're inside
the CDC, taken it over.

MEADOWS
(Earnestly) If we talk positive, Mister
President, everyone will think positive.
We're winning and we have to make that case,
keep telling people that we're winning.

TRUMP
Exactly. Exactly what I've said. We're
winning. We're beating it. We're doing much
better fighting this virus than any other
country. Our numbers are much better. We've
got to be upbeat, make sure there's no
panic. We've got to look to the positive,
take the wind out of Biden hiding behind
that mask, and get through this thing. The
election is the most important thing now.
We've got tremendous, tremendous momentum
and need to keep that up. I want the Vice
President to make what we've done more
visible. That'd be a good use of him.

MEADOWS
He's scheduled for the Mayo Clinic end of
this week, Sir.

TRUMP
Good. Very good. Make sure it's fully
covered. And by our people. Don't let the
fake media screw it up.

BLACKOUT.

MEADOWS
(In the dark.) Yes, Sir. We'll get that
done.

LIGHTS UP ON MAYO HOSPITAL HALLWAY WITH A
TIGHT CLUSTER OF PHYSICIANS SHOWING **VICE
PRESIDENT PENCE** THE FACILITIES. PROMINENT
SIGN IN BACKGROUND: "FACEMASKS REQUIRED IN
THIS AREA." ALL BUT PENCE ARE MASKED.

> (Instrumental: Overture to opera
> *William Tell*, by Rossini.)
>
> (Gesturing and pointing, PHYSICIANS
> and PENCE move en masse across stage,
> past a pair of hospital **ATTENDANTS**
> fully draped and masked in their
> PPE.)
>
> (Instrumental reaches "Lone Ranger"
> section of the overture.)

ATTENDANT ONE
Who was that unmasked man?

ATTENDANT TWO
He's the Vice President. Came to visit, I
understand.

ATTENDANT ONE
Show and tell? What doesn't HE understand???

> (Instrumental music continues for a
> few beats then ends abruptly in mid
> phrase.)

BLACKOUT.

LIGHTS UP ON OVAL OFFICE. TRUMP IS AT DESK
LOOKING AT A NEWS BROADCAST, AMERICAN FLAG
PROMINENT TO ONE SIDE

VOICE ON COMMUNICATOR
The Vice President, Sir.

TRUMP
All right. I'll have him. (Turns from TV to
face door, rising laboriously.)

- 63 -

(PENCE enters; they shake hands.)

TRUMP
How did it go, Mike? Looking good?

PENCE
Looking very good, Sir. They appreciated
knowing they have your full support. I made
sure to —

TRUMP
Did they appreciate our help in getting this
under control? The White House's help, I
mean.

(TRUMP sits behind desk.)

PENCE
(Still standing) That, too. Yes, Sir. I
expressed to them that —

TRUMP
Have you seen the reports? (Motions at TV
screen) On Fox, Mike?

PENCE
No, Sir. Not today. No, Sir.

TRUMP
Well, despite the CDC's lack of discipline,
and despite Fauci's and Redfield's sour
reports, we're winning. In fact we've won,
we've beaten it. As far as this COVID thing
goes, we've prevailed.

PENCE
We're winning. We won. We've prevailed.
We've —

TRUMP
That'll do, Pence. This is another example
of why I'll be judged a great president, one
of the greatest. I'm what America has
lacked, what it's needed for a long time.

And we're going to make sure that word gets
out very clearly. The greatest. Very loud
and very clear. Ali used to say that all the
time, and he was right.

TRUMP
"AMERICA FIRST"

(Based upon "Largo al Factotum,"
Figaro's First Act aria in Rossini's
Barber of Seville.)

America first, yes. America first.
America first, yes. America first.

The best president, there's much that I
have done. Yes. Much.
America. America. America first!
In my next four years, there's much
more to do. Yes, much.
America. America. America first!

(TRUMP stands)

I work more than anyone.
I work day and night. I work day and
night.
To make this country great again, great
again.

The greatest, that's Trump, that is I,
that is so true.
America. America. America. First!
That the country is lucky to have found
me is fact, so true.
America first! America first!
The country is lucky to have found me.
So true.

The country is lucky to have found me.
So true.
America first! America! America!
America first!

Ready for anything,
Expert in most things,
There's little with which I can't cope.
So rich in experience,
With so many problems I've solved,
There's nothing that is beyond my
scope.

Whether it's our borders
Or the environment,
I'm the one who's in control.
Unlike poor Europe,
We don't lack for energy.
We can always go back to coal.

In business I'm skilled. Also in
negotiation.
Loved in the cities, in the suburbs as
well.
Those on the coasts show their support
for me.
In the heartland, my rallies continue
to swell.
For me!

America knows what it had lacked.
In the fall they'll send me back.
They'll want me back,
A leader who knows how to lead, who
leads.

(Walks toward flag)

Everyone wants me. Everyone loves me.
The men, and the women; the young, and
the old.
Those on the border, those on the
coasts.
Those where the sun's hot, those where
it's cold.
Everyone wants me. Everyone loves me.
The men and the women; the young and
the old.
Those on the border, those on the
coasts.
Those where the sun's hot, those where
it's cold.

(TRUMP embraces fluttering flag)

America, America.
America, America, America, America,
America, America.
America!

(TRUMP turns back from flag.)

Always a crowd. Always excitement.
It's always Trump they yell, Trump they
want, want above all.
Trump above all, me above all.
It's always Trump they want. It's
always Trump they want.
It's always Trump they want; it's me
above all.

(Briskly) *I curbed China. Brought their thievery to an end.*
I met with Kim in Korea. Made of him a friend.
Brought back jobs, despite COVID's nasty break,
Calmed the MidEast, where the future is at stake,
Sat with friends abroad to say we won't be ruled,
Faced enemies near and far to show we won't be fooled.
I am the President of this America and It's for America that I stand.
America first! America first! America first! America first!

(Rapidly) *Yes, I am the one. I've done so much.*
There's much yet to do.
As much as I've done, there's much yet to do.
So much yet left to do.
As much as I've done, there's much yet to do.
Four more years! I'll make us great again!
Yes, I'm the one!
None's done so much. But there's much left to do.
As much as I've done, there's much yet to do.
So much yet left to do.

(Normal pace) *I've done so much, but
there's much left to do.
As much as I've done, there's much yet
to do.
So much yet left ...
So much left
To do!*

> (TRUMP peers out over audience, hands
> on hips during an instrumental
> reprise. Slowly he folds his arms
> across his chest and elevates his
> chin. Pence moves close and feebly
> tries to imitate the gesture.)

STAGE LIGHTS DIM TO DARK AS MUSIC ENDS.

AT LIGHTS UP, DOCTOR FAUCI IS ON LARGE
MONITOR SCREEN, AGAIN BEING INTERVIEWED.

INTERVIEWER
(Unseen) Could you tell us, finally, Doctor
Fauci, how you would characterize our
progress dealing with COVID here?

FAUCI
The death toll continues to rise, I'm
afraid. We're not at the end of this yet.
And maybe not for quite a while. We're going
in the wrong direction. The numbers don't
look good and I'm very concerned. In fact,
I'm not satisfied with what's going on. The
summer weather may not bring as much relief
as we might expect with typical flu. It
might make for a worse situation. We'll need
to be prudent. We'd be wise to be cautious.
Everyone should be more cautious.

MONITOR OFF THEN BLACKOUT.

TRUMP
They're right you know. This COVID thing has
been greatly exaggerated. No worse than the
flu but the Democrats think they can use it
to spoil my reelection.

KUSHNER
We'll get that under control very soon, Sir.
But the protests and anarchy are getting
violent. Lots of property damage.

HICKS
Because of that George Floyd thing, mainly.

BARR
Local law enforcement hasn't been very
effective. They're just letting it go on in
many cities. It may be time to get our
people in there to preserve order.

TRUMP
What about here? Anything going on here, in
D.C.?

MCENANY
Yes, Sir. I'm afraid there are protesters
gathering anywhere they can get their media
coverage.

HICKS
Protestors are outside the White House right
now.

TRUMP
Is it dangerous? Are they going to try to
storm the White House?

                            BARR
No, Sir. We're well protected here. They
couldn't storm a government building.

                          MCENANY
But it is bad optics, Mister President. We
should issue a statement to get ahead of it.

                           TRUMP
(To Barr) You sure about that, Bill? Maybe I
should go to the bunker.

                            BARR
That's not necessary, Sir. I assure you
there's no danger.

                           HICKS
I think, Mister President, that you should
make a brief public statement in the Rose
Garden. Something positive for the nation.
Then, as you proposed, you can walk calmly
across to Saint John's to show that you're
in control, that law and order still
prevail.

                           TRUMP
Fine idea. Fine. Let's take a look at that
bunker first. I want to be sure everything
is ready in case I need it.

          (TRUMP in the lead, all exit stage
          right.)

BRIEFLY BLACKOUT.

LIGHTS UP ON MIXED CROWD OF MEN AND WOMEN,
OLD AND YOUNG, BLACK AND WHITE, CLUSTERED AT
STAGE LEFT. BANNERS AND PLACARDS FEATURE
PICTURES OF GEORGE FLOYD. OTHER BLACK LIVES
MATTER SENTIMENTS ARE PROMINENT.

          (Crowd silently marches across stage
          gesturing, waving the banners and
          placards, exiting right.)

                          - 71 -

BLACKOUT.

LIGHTS UP ON WHITE HOUSE ROSE GARDEN. TRUMP
AT LECTERN FACING OUT. MIXED CROWD OF STAFF
AND ADVISORS (ABOVE) PLUS GUESTS. ONLY A
VERY FEW ARE MASKED.

                    TRUMP
I am your president of law and order and an
ally of all peaceful protestors.

          (Sounds of angry crowds, pops and
          flashes of light from crowd control
          grenades. Sound of batons beating
          against shields, people coughing and
          yelling from offstage. Smoke of tear
          gas drifts onto stage.)

                    TRUMP
It's important that we dominate the streets.
There must be an end to rioting, looting,
and wanton destruction. These are being
allowed by the Democratic mayors and
governors. But not by me. Now, I am going to
pay my respects to a very, very special
place.

          (TRUMP leaves lectern and joins his
          staff.)

                    TRUMP
(To Barr) Everything okay out there, Bill?

                    BARR
Being taken care of as we speak, Sir.

          (TRUMP strides toward stage right.
          BARR, HOPE HICKS, KAYLEIGH MCENANY,
          JARED KUSHNER, MARK MEADOWS, **STEPHEN
          MILLER, MARK MILLEY** and others
          accompany him behind.)

SCENE GRADUALLY CHANGES (OR ROTATES) TO THE
APPROACH TO ST. JOHNS. LINGERING HINTS OF
SMOKE.

TRUMP AT BASE OF STEPS OF ST. JOHNS. THE
CHURCH PASTOR, RIGHT REV. MARIANN BUDDE, IS
IN FULL CLERICAL DRESS FAR UPSTAGE.

> (TRUMP turns out, fumbles with bible
> as he attempts to hold it up for the
> photo op. Camera flashes prominent
> amidst instrumental triumphal
> chords.)

> (RR BUDDE silently shakes head in
> disapproval.)

BLACKOUT.

LIGHTS UP ON OVAL OFFICE, TRUMP WITH CHIEF
OF STAFF MEADOWS.

TRUMP
What are we going to do about that ramp
thing, Mark? Have you seen how CNN and those
other trash outlets keep showing the same
clip over and over. They're making a big,
big deal about nothing. Nothing. It was a
very, very steep ramp. Steep and slippery.
No one would want to fall on that steep and
slippery ramp. It's a shame those fake media
people can be so disrespectful. They create
so many ways to make me look bad. They
shouldn't do that. I don't do that. I never
do that.

MEADOWS
No, Sir. Only when it's well deserved.

TRUMP
Exactly. When it's very, very well deserved.
I should be used to it by now. They made fun
of all the great leaders. Like with
Roosevelt's metal braces and Lincoln's big

- 73 -

frame, that white sheet Gandhi always wore, Churchill's Vee and cigar, Hitler's Chaplin mustache. That kind of thing.

MEADOWS
It might be better not to make that last comparison so specific, Mister President.

TRUMP
(Pause) I see what you mean. Hitler wasn't great. He was a terrible, terrible person. Don't quote me on that. (Mischievous grin.) What he did to the Jews was terrible. But the media makes fun of all the great and powerful people. It's what they do. It's how they make their money.

MEADOWS
Sir, if I may, it's obvious what you mean to say, but some might take advantage, pick out a word or two and put on a negative spin.

TRUMP
Crazy Nancy would. Pelosi and her gang always find a way to make something good look bad. Never mind. But about that ramp thing. And the drink, the water glass thing. That's all fiction. Total fiction. Look (pacing deliberately), it was the ramp, not me. I'm walking just fine! Such a foolish, fake story about that ramp.

TRUMP
"JUST FINE AS YOU CAN SEE"
It was slippery. It wasn't me.
I was careful. Had a right to be.
I'm walking, just fine as you can see.
It was a steep ramp, so I took my time.

I walked slow. Anyone would do the same.
Now I'm walking, just fine as you can see.

Fake media goes nuts when their well runs dry.
How deep will they dig for their next lie?
I could make them pay. I am not shy.
My people have my back, I needn't try.

It was slippery. That wasn't me.
I was careful. I was right to be.
Now I'm walking, just fine as you can see.

> (TRUMP lifts water glass from tray on desk. He takes a sip Academy "squared" style.)

And that silliness about the water glass???

Glass too full. Someone else's mistake.
Had to lift it slow. Hand couldn't shake.
I'm drinking, just fine as you can see.

Up to the brim, it was ready to spill,
Had to be careful that it didn't tilt.
Now I'm drinking, just fine as you can see.

Fake media goes nuts when their well
runs dry.
How deep will they dig for their next
lie?
I could make them pay. I am not shy.
My people have my back, I needn't try.

I'm walking, as you can see.
I'm drinking, as you can see.
Walking and drinking, just fine as you
can see.

BLACKOUT.

LIGHTS UP SLOWLY IN A WARM RED. IT'S DEEP
INTO SUMMER.

STAGE RIGHT: (**OLD CHORUS**) CROWD OF MIDDLE
AGED TO SENIOR PEOPLE, CASUALLY DRESSED, IN
QUIET CONVERSATION. MOST ARE MASKED.

STAGE LEFT: (**YOUNG CHORUS**) CROWD OF YOUNG
PEOPLE IN SHORTS AND CUTOFFS, MOVING ABOUT
ENERGETICALLY. VERY FEW ARE MASKED.

WARM LIGHTING FAVORS YOUNG CHORUS.

YOUNG CHORUS
"STUCK HERE IN THE CITY"
Hot town. Stuck here in the city.
Everythin's closed. It's gettin' pretty
shitty.
No job, so mom'll show some pity,
Says that she'll drop off a pot of
ziti.

Nothing comin' in except for
unemployment.
Hard to sell stuff; everyone's savings
have been spent.

Days are bad, but the nights are worse.
Hopin' it'll get better has been a
curse.
Hangin' with our buds used to be allll
right.
Not so much fun when we're stuck in the
same plight.

So, man, you know that it's a pity.
No money. Stuck here where we are.
Unemployed, in the city.
Waiting for word, in the city.

Used to be fun. Had a little money.
Dressed up fine and spent evenin's with
a honey.
Ate out, feeling mighty spiffy.
But that was before even rent was
gettin' iffy.
Now all I do is wait on the man to
call.
Hopin' to hear that I should come in
after all.

Days are bad, but the nights are worse.
Hopin' it'll get better has been a
curse.

Hangin' with our buds used to be allll
right.
Not so much fun when we share the same
plight.

Yeah, man, you know that it's a pity.
No money. Stuck here where we are,
Unemployed, in the city.
Waiting for word, in the city.

Hot town, and stuck here in the city.
Everythin's closed. It's gettin' pretty
shitty.
No job, so mom'll show some pity,
Says that she'll drop off a pot of
ziti.
Nothing comin' in except for
unemployment.
Hard to sell stuff 'cause everyone's
savings have been spent.

Days are bad, but the nights are worse.
Hopin' it'll get better has been a
curse.
Hangin' with our buds used to be allll
right.
Not so much fun when we share the same
plight.

So, man, you know that it's a pity.
No money. Stuck here where we are.
Unemployed, in the city.
Waiting for word, in the city.
(Fade)
Unemployed, in the city.

Waiting for word, in the city.
Unemployed, in the city.
Waiting for word, in the city.

(YOUNG CHORUS goes static.)

<u>WARM LIGHTING FAVORS OLD CHORUS.</u>

OLD CHORUS
"IT'D BE NICE TO GET OUT OF THIS TOWN"
Seeing dark store fronts isn't pretty.
People in line to get free food.
It's a shock to the eyes, not good.
Not good.

We've spent our entire lives in this
city.
We're as much it, as it is ours.
Must admit though, it's nicer with less
cars.
Safer. But ...

It'd be nice to get out of this town.
Go to Vermont or maybe to Maine.
The trick is to find a good place to
go.
The competition for rentals is simply
insane.
It's insane.
It's insane.

Wish we could plan on when this'd be
over.
The heat of the summer makes everything
worse.

*It's hard to accept that it must just
run its course.
The future? Short futures.*

*Miss Liberty has gray clouds above her.
All the violence is such a shame.
But it's natural to want to place the
blame.
Too much stress.*

*It'd be wise to get out of this town.
Find a village where we can relax.
Problem is everywhere else's locked
down.
All they want to see of us is our
backs.*

*Stress. Too much stress.
Must go somewhere. Somewhere.*

*Time for us to get out of this town.
Go to Vermont or maybe to Maine.
The trick is to find the right place to
go.
The competition for rentals is simply
insane.*

*(More emotional) We have to get out of
this town.
Go to Vermont or maybe to Maine.
But we can't find a decent place to go.
The competition for rentals is simply
insane.
Insane. Insane. Insane.*

(Old chorus goes static.)

<u>LIGHTS BRIGHTEN, STILL WARM TONED, AS
CHORUSES MINGLE.</u>

MINGLED CHORUSES
"WE'RE HAVING A PANDEMIC"
(YOUNG:) *We're havin' a pandemic,*
A damn Chinese pandemic.
Everything is closed here,
We thirst for our next beer.
We certainly ask: Why mask?

We're lookin' for work still.
It's clear we can't pay bills.
Everyone thinks it'll end soon,
But that's just D.C.'s tune.
In the meantime we ask: Why mask?

Oh, the misery.
Shut shops are all we see.
How long must this shit be?

(OLD:) *We're caught in a pandemic.*
Yes, a frightening pandemic.
Our friends are all dying.
D.C.'s barely trying.
It's an easy task. Please mask.

China started this pandemic.
Viruses for them are endemic.
There's not much else we can do,
So we suggest this to you:
It's an easy task. Please mask.

The world's gone dull these days.
Our families stay away.
Are we alone to stay?

(YOUNG//OLD): This mess has gotten old.
Have patience is what we're told.
That's easy if you (are)//(aren't) old.

(YOUNG:) We're havin' a pandemic,
A damn Chinese pandemic.
Everything is closed here,
We thirst for our next beer.
We certainly ask: Why mask?

(OLD:) We're caught in a pandemic.
Yes, a frightening pandemic.
Our friends are all dying,
D.C.'s barely trying.
It's an easy task. Please mask.

(YOUNG//OLD): This mess has gotten old.
Have patience we are told.
That's easy if you (are)//(aren't) old.

(YOUNG:) We certainly ask: Why mask?
(OLD:) It's an easy task. Please mask.

(YOUNG//OLD fade together, so as to be
confusing:)
We certainly ask: Why mask? //
    It's an easy task. Please mask.
We certainly ask: Why mask? //
    It's an easy task. Please mask.

LIGHTS FADE THROUGH DEEP RED TO BLACKOUT.

<u>LIGHTS UP ON NETWORK CONVENTION COVERAGE.</u>
<u>CNN READERS ONE AND TWO</u> <u>AT DESK STAGE RIGHT.</u>
<u>FOX READERS ONE AND TWO</u> <u>AT DESK STAGE LEFT.</u>

<u>LIGHTS FAVOR CNN DESK.</u>

CNN READER ONE
These are unusual times. With no let up in
the COVID situation, there'll be no crowds,
no floor celebration.

CNN READER TWO
That's true. Both nominating conventions
will be essentially virtual. The Democrats
are first up. Next week it will be the
Republicans' turn. It'll be interesting how
this all works out.

CNN READER ONE
Despite some drama and the political
posturing of the huge initial field of
Democratic candidates, there's really no
doubt now who'll be each party's candidate.
Takes a bit of the fun and mystery out of
the process, doesn't it?

CNN READER TWO
It does. What we CAN count on is that this
is the true start of the campaign season.
There's a lot of fireworks to look forward
to.

CNN READER ONE
And to a lot of money being spent. Both the
Democratic and Republican party people will
be looking to rally open the donor spigots.

CNN READER TWO
"Rally open." I like that. Yes, money's
going to be the key from here on.

<u>LIGHTS FADE AND SHIFT TO FAVOR FOX DESK.</u>

FOX READER ONE
We can't expect to hear anything new over
the next few days. Most of the attention
will be on how strongly Kamala Harris can
project herself and if she can breathe some
life into a ticket headed by Biden.

FOX READER TWO
And maybe a little life into Biden himself.
"Sleepy Joe" is rather unsporting of Trump,
but it's not a bad slam. (He chuckles.)
That's Trump.

FOX READER ONE
He has a talent for nasty nicknames. And
isn't shy.

FOX READER TWO
(Chuckling) Not shy at all. But yes, it'll
be more of what we've heard before, with
some mods now that there's a single real
contender. Distinctions without a
difference, though.

FOX READER ONE
Quite a flock of bright and not so bright
stars scheduled to appear, one way or
another. Both sides have their choir. Still,
it should be a close race, I would say.

FOX READER TWO
Probably so, and a matter of money from here
on, who has the bucks to use the media more
effectively, who can reach out and capture
the most undecided folks.

LIGHTS UP EVENLY. READERS LOOK EARNESTLY OUT
AT AUDIENCE.

READERS QUARTET
"MOOLAH, MOOLAH"

*Presidential hopefuls sing this song -
moolah! moolah!
Candidates' races run all year long -
moolah, they all say.
They craft their pleas to make them
hard to ignore - for moolah, moolah.
A little bit of fear always brings in
more - yes, moolah is what they say.*

*Need to campaign all day.
Need to campaign all night.
The one with the money to run the
biggest ads,
Is more likely to carry the fight.*

*No matter which party, running takes
much dough - moolah, moolah!
Always hammering out the message for
people they don't know - moolah is the
way.
No matter what the issue, all must pay
to play - so moolah, moolah.
Set the stakes in black and white, no
issue can be gray - moolah will win the
day.*

*Need to campaign all day.
Need to campaign all night.
The one with the money to saturate the
screens
Is more likely to carry the fight.*

Campaign coffers have grown so rich -
with moolah, moolah.
They pay big staffs to refine and
promote their pitch - moolah helps them
say.
Every voter hopes that their side wins
- so send in moolah, moolah.
Fulfilling a few promises covers many
sins - moolah paves the way.

Need to campaign all day.
Need to campaign all night.
The one with the money to make his
message soar
Is more likely to carry the fight.

No one admits that money does it all -
moolah, moolah.
But it'll make the difference when
summer turns to fall - moolah sure will
work.
So they keep the pressure high even
when catering to their crowd - with
moolah, moolah.
Say it very often and say it very loud
- moolah will pave the way.

Need to campaign all day.
Need to campaign all night.
The one with the money to run the
biggest ads,
Is more likely to carry the fight.
Whoever has the money for the biggest
ads,
Is more likely to carry the fight. Yes!

BLACKOUT.

LIGHTS UP ON VIRTUAL DEMOCRATIC PARTY
CONVENTION IN MILWAUKEE. WELL SPACED GROUP
OF LIFE-SIZE 2D FIGURES SPAN THE STAGE, ALL
WITH ATTACHED CLOTH MASKS. POLITICAL
PLACARDS ARE SCATTERED AMONG THESE. REAR
WALL IS COVERED WITH BUNTING AND POLITICAL
BANNERS.

MIDSTAGE RIGHT: A HIGHLIGHTED LECTERN SET AT
THE FRONT EDGE OF A PODIUM. IN SEQUENCE, A
NUMBER OF RECOGNIZABLE FIGURES MOMENTARILY
STAND BEHIND IT, WITH A BRIEF BRIGHT FLASH
THEN MOMENT OF DARKNESS TO OBSCURE EACH
ENTRANCE AND EXIT. NONE SPEAK.

FLASH: BERNIE SANDERS AT LECTERN, WITH HIS
DISTINCTIVE STOOP AND WIDE ARM SALUTE.

FLASH: A TALL, BROADLY SMILING MICHELLE
OBAMA AT LECTERN.

FLASH: WHITE-HAIRED BILL CLINTON AT LECTERN.

> (CLINTON incongruously looks about,
> nods a shaky head.)

FLASH: A DIFFERENT LECTERN, NOW SANS PODIUM,
IS HIGHLIGHTED. **NANCY PELOSI** ENTERS.

> (PELOSI stares straight out as she
> silently mouths words of a speech.
> She gestures as she mimes
> determination then pauses.)

PELOSI
President Trump was impeached for good
cause. He was acquitted. But it was a
meaningless, political acquittal, which came
after no witnesses were called, no documents
presented. There remains much that his
administration must answer for, that it has

failed to address, that now must be addressed.

(PELOSI raises one hand.)

Who is standing in the way? Mitch McConnell.

(PELOSI raises the other hand.)

Who is standing in the way? Donald Trump.

(PELOSI raises both hands.)

Who is standing in the way? Mitch McConnell and Donald Trump!

(PELOSI clasps her hands together.)

Until November!!!

FLASH: A YET DIFFERENT LECTERN IS HIGHLIGHTED. **HILLARY CLINTON,** IN WHITE PANTSUIT, STANDS BEHIND.

HILLARY
It has been four years. "I didn't realize how dangerous he was," they have said to me, some with tears in their eyes. "I wish I could go back and do it over," they have said. And what did HE say? "Drain the swamp!" he said. (She laughs aloud.) Lobbyists are wallowing in his swamp and shaping his campaign! They love his swamp, are growing rich in it. (She laughs aloud again.) I have been asked many times: "What went wrong?" Clearly, we didn't work hard enough. We need to work harder this time. And what did HE ask of the nation? "What do you have to lose," he asked. The answer to that is just as clear: Far more than we imagined.

STAGE LIGHTS SLOWLY DIM. FLASH: A YET
DIFFERENT LECTERN IS HIGHLIGHTED. KAMALA
HARRIS STANDS BEHIND.

HARRIS
The constant chaos leaves us adrift. The
incompetence makes us feel afraid. The
callousness makes us feel alone. We can do
better. But, make no mistake, the road ahead
will not be easy.

FLASH: A TALL, LEAN, GRAYING BARACK OBAMA
STANDS BEHIND LECTERN.

OBAMA
This isn't a normal convention.... It's not
a normal time.... But here's the thing:
Believe in your own ability. Embrace your
own responsibility ... as citizens.... Make
sure that the basic tenets of our democracy
endure.

FLASH: **JOE BIDEN** ENTERS BRISKLY FROM STAGE
RIGHT, TAKING OFF HIS BLUE, CLOTH FACEMASK
AS HE DOES SO. HE STANDS BEHIND A LECTERN AT
STAGE RIGHT AND SMILES OUT.

BIDEN
The current president has cloaked America in
darkness for much too long. Now history has
delivered us into a perfect storm, one of
the most difficult moments America has ever
faced. A time of real peril. This is our
moment to make hope and history rhyme.

LIGHTS DIM.

BIDEN
Yes, friends. Realize that this is our
moment to make hope and history rhyme.

> (BIDEN puts up both hands, index
> fingers upright like goal posts. He
> stands motionless.)

<u>HILLARY CLINTON</u> REAPPEARS, BRIGHTLY
<u>ISOLATED, AT THE TOP OF A VERY TALL PLATFORM</u>
<u>AT STAGE LEFT.</u>

>(HILLARY looks down at audience.)

HILLARY

I wish Donald Trump had been a better
president. Yes, "What do you have to lose,"
he did ask. Now we know, because we have
come close to losing it. Joe Biden must win.
But as Kamala Harris said: "... the road
ahead will not be easy."

>(HILLARY looks at the static Biden
>and addresses him directly.)

You must win.

HILLARY
"THE PAIN OF LOSS"

(Intensely operatic, angry)
The pain of loss had overwhelmed me.
I could not believe, how great
Was the chance that I had missed.
Ohh, the chance I missed.

Now it's come to you.
This deceiver known as Trump must be
defeated.
This deceiver known as Trump must be
defeated.

If you should fail, the Democratic
party will go pale.
If you should fail, Democracy could be
lost.

Democracy itself could be lost.

Democracy could be lost, if you should fail.

      (Instrumental)

You'll be blamed as I was.
You'll be shamed as I was.
Blamed and shamed as I was.
Democracy's bright shine bedimmed.
Scorned. By history. And forgotten.
Democracy's bright shine lost.

Yes, democracy will be no more,
No more, if by you
This Trump is not defeated.

Joe! Joe! Joe!!
You must be fierce.
Don't fail as did I.

HILLARY'S HIGHLIGHT GRADUALLY DIMS TO OFF AS
THE PLATFORM RECEDES.

(BIDEN, reanimated, lowers hands to
grasp lectern. He glances to his left
and up, then speaks earnestly.)

BIDEN
I thank all of you — campaign staff,
energetic workers, supporters — for bringing
us to this moment. Needed more than ever, it
will be our solemn task to regain the White
House and heal our country.

Here's the thing: Most Americans see the
truth and are eager for a change in
leadership. Trump is strangling democracy.
He wants to silence your voices any way he
can. We've a lot to overcome. As Kamala
Harris said: "... the road ahead will not be
easy."

BIDEN
"VOTES WON'T COME EASY"
Blue votes won't come easy,
It's clear they won't come easy.
Blue votes won't come easy,
It's clear they won't come easy.

You've seen I've paid my dues and it's
not some breaking news
That Blue votes won't come easy.

But Democrats must get out and make our
win a rout,
Even though that won't be easy.

*Keep the past in mind and all of
Trump's misdeeds.
The future is ours to mold,
Remember, big oaks come from little
seeds.*

*We need to do so much, I'm asking for
your trust.
A departing Trump is what we must see.
That hope of mine has been growing a
long time,
Though winning won't be easy.*

*So roll up your sleeves and work
together.
Make sure your friends come out and
vote,
So our republic's freed from Trump's
cruel tether.*

(Instrumental continues.)

Here's the thing.

*You know I've paid my dues and it's not
some breaking news
That Blue votes won't come easy.
You must get out and make our win a
rout,
Though we know that won't be easy.*

*Keep the past in mind and all of
Trump's misdeeds.
The future is ours to mold.
Remember, a new vision is what we do
need.*

- 93 -

We need to do so much, I'm praying for
your trust,
So that a departing Trump is what we
see.
This hope of mine has been growing a
long time,
Though winning won't be easy.

So tell all you know, Trump's rule must
now go.
Make sure your friends come out and
vote,
So we can have that bright tomorrow.

We need to do so much, so I'm asking
for your trust.
Make sure your friends come out and
vote,
So we can have that bright tomorrow.

LINGERING LIGHT ON BIDEN.

BLACKOUT.

LIGHTS UP ON WASHINGTON DC'S MELLON
AUDITORIUM, DEVOID OF PEOPLE. THE SURROUND
INCLUDES UPLIT FLUTED PILLARS, MANY AMERICAN
FLAGS, WITH A HUGE FLAG HANGING ON WALL
BEHIND.

REAR STAGE RIGHT: VERY LARGE MONITOR SCREEN,
DARK.

CENTER STAGE: BROAD PODIUM EDGED WITH STARS
AND A HIGHLIGHTED LECTERN ADORNED WITH A
THREE LINE SIGN: "TRUMP - PENCE - MAKE
AMERICA GREAT AGAIN." AS ABOVE, THE SERIAL
PRESENTATION OF SPEAKERS AT LECTERN USES A

BRIGHT FLASH AND MOMENT OF DARKNESS BETWEEN
EACH, TO OBSCURE THEIR ENTRY/EXIT. OTHER
SPEAKERS APPEAR ON THE MONITOR.

LECTERN HIGHLIGHT DIMS, MONITOR BRIGHTENS.

      (Rep. **JIM JORDAN** on monitor, in shirt
      sleeves with tie.)

                   JORDAN
The Republican Party is the pro-America
party. President Trump is the pro-America
candidate. I love this President's
intensity.

Democrats won't let you go to school, but
they'll let you go loot. America needs
President Trump to fight their crazy ideas.
And that's why I'm busting my tail to help
President Trump get reelected. We need him.

JORDAN FADES BUT MONITOR STAYS LIT.

FLASH: NIKKI HALEY, IN BRIGHT PINK, STANDS
BEHINDS LECTERN.

                   HALEY
President Trump is leading a new era of
opportunity. Our economy needs him. Joe
Biden (tilts head to right) and the
Socialist Left would be a disaster.

Joe Biden is good for Iran and ISIS, great
for Communist China, and (tilts head to
left) a godsend to everyone who wants
America to apologize, abstain, and abandon
our values.

You know you want President Trump.

FLASH: DONALD J. TRUMP, JR. APPEARS AT
LECTERN.

TRUMP, JR.
Joe Biden is the Loch Ness Monster of the
Swamp. He and the radical Left are coming
for our freedom of speech, to have it be the
"Silenced Majority."

Anarchists have been flooding our streets.
(Voice rising) This election is church,
work, and school versus rioting, looting,
and vandalism, what Biden and the Democrats
call "peaceful protesting." Our people don't
do that!

(Sugary) I love my dad. But more than that,
he's done a fantastic job. I was fortunate
to be his son. You can have the world that
Donald Trump and the Republican Party are
after. Give him an overwhelming vote of
confidence for ANOTHER! FOUR! YEARS! (Big
smile)

FLASH: RAND PAUL STANDS BEHIND LECTERN.

PAUL
President Trump is the first president in a
generation to seek to end war rather than
start one (raises both hands slightly). Our
occasional policy differences are outweighed
by our agreements. Compared with the
disastrous record of Joe Biden (raises one
finger) we need President Trump.

Fight the Socialists who are poisoning our
schools and burning our cities. Join me in
believing in and supporting President Trump.
(Raises both hands and goes very still.)

FLASH: HALEY, TRUMP JR., AND PAUL BEHIND
LECTERN.

Vote for him, vote for him, vote for him.

When he speaks believe him, believe him, believe him.

We believe in him,
Believe in whatever he may say.
Whatever he declaims or tweets out,
There's nothing we can't justify.
He speaks for the G.O.P.

We need him, we need him, we need him.
His tweets reach so many, so many, so many.
His core is fiercely loyal, so loyal, so loyal.
It's support that we can count on, can count on, can count on.

We have ambitious plans.
Obviously we aim to rise far above.
In him we can have that potent ally,
If we'll give him that abundant love.
His base is a treasure trove.

(MONITOR BRIGHTENS AND JORDAN APPEARS.

JORDAN
(Asynchronously with the trio.)
I tell you that want him, I want him, I want him.
No matter his flaws I want him, I want him, I want him.

- 97 -

Like me, he gets the crowd excited,
excited, excited.
His support is for me to draw from, to
draw from, to draw from.

HALEY, TRUMP JR., PAUL
(As above) We want him, we want him, we
want him.
No fault will lead us to abandon,
abandon, abandon.
His conspiracy claims are so strange,
so strange, so strange.
Still, there's method in having him
rant on, rant on, rant on.

There's reason for us to want him.
We see how he's touched a populist
chord.
On his coattails we therefore will
ride,
Help ourselves to succeed by aping his
every word.
It's best to be on board.

We love him, we love him, we love him.
No matter what flaws, we love him, we
love him, we love him.
He gets the crowd excited, excited,
excited.
His support is for us to draw from, to
draw from, to draw from.

Our futures are tied to his,
Tied to his since the party has given in.
While when alone we may disagree,
In public we'll nod yes, we'll parrot him.
Why crawl out on a limb?

JORDAN
(Again, asynchronously with the trio below)
Because the truth is that I need him,
I'll love him, I'll use him.
His tweets reach so many, so many, so many.
His core has been so loyal, so loyal, so loyal.
It's support that I can count on, can count on, can count on.
Vote for him, vote for him, vote for him. (repeat ad lib)

HALEY, TRUMP JR., PAUL
Because we need him, we'll love him, we want him.
His tweets reach so many, so many, so many.
His core has been so loyal, so loyal, so loyal.
It's support that we can count on, can count on, can count on.
Vote for him, vote for him, vote for him. (repeat ad lib)

JORDAN, ON MONITOR, AND TRIO GO STATIC IN
MID-PHRASE,

BLACKOUT.

LIGHTS UP ON LECTERN WITH NO ONE BEHIND.
MONITOR LIT BUT BLANK. AFTER A PAUSE, POMPEO
APPEARS ON MONITOR, LOOKING TO ONE SIDE AS
IF HE BELIEVES HE HAS DISPLACED SOMEONE.

> (Brief snatch of music: Humming main
> title theme from *Moses the Lawgiver*.)

POMPEO
I am here, in Israel, Jehovah's land. The
land of Moses, who had, as has our President
Trump, done so much to promote and ensure
the freedom of his people. I ... (Static and
visual noise.) ... When he visited he was,
as he said, welcomed like the "King of
Israel," like the "second coming of God." He
... (More Static and visual noise on
monitor.)

POMPEO'S IMAGE FREEZES. MONITOR IMAGE
BECOMES TOTALLY PIXILATED. MUSIC ENDS.
SCREEN GOES DARK.

BACKOUT.

LIGHTS UP ON BRICK EXTERIOR OF FT. MCHENRY.
MANY AMERICAN POLE FLAGS AT STAGE REAR.

MIKE PENCE, SUITED AND WEARING A RED TIE, IS
AT LECTERN SET UPON A PODIUM EDGED IN STARS.
LIGHTING RENDERS HIM VIRTUALLY COLORLESS,
EXCEPT FOR THE TIE. HE LOOKS OUT OVER THE
VICE PRESIDENTIAL SEAL, NODDING AND SMILING
TO A VARIED ASSEMBLY THAT, THEIR BACKS TO
AUDIENCE, ARE APPLAUDING. IN ADDITION TO MEN
AND WOMEN OF VARIOUS AGES, THERE ARE PEOPLE
IN UNIFORM, YOUNG CHILDREN, PEOPLE WITH
WALKERS AND WHEELCHAIRS. A VERY FEW ARE

MASKED, SOME WITH THEM DOWN UPON THEIR
CHINS.

> (Applause fades. PENCE nods and
> offers a tight smile.)

PENCE
Democrats spent four days attacking America.
They want to end the American experiment,
crush its ideals and its promise. (Pause for
applause) Biden says he wants to lead but he
has been wrong on nearly every major foreign
policy and national security issue over the
past four decades. You will not be safe in
Joe Biden's America. He's a Trojan horse for
the radical Left. (Pause for applause) He
and the Democrats' aims are to deprive our
people of its freedom and prosperity and
security.

> (He grips lectern with both hands.)

We will reelect our President and principled
Republican leaders across the land. With
God's help, we will make America strong
again, again. Let us fix our eyes on the
author and perfecter of our faith and our
freedom and never forget that where the
spirit of the Lord is, there is freedom. We
need President Trump to lead us for four
more years, to fulfill his promise to us and
America's promise to the world.

> (Heavy gospel music bass beat
> starts.)

PENCE
"HE'LL TAKE YOU THERE"
(Swaying slightly.)
I know a place
Where everybody smiles. Yes.
Where nobody is worried. No.

Where no one lies, no, no,
Lies to hopeful faces.

Vote Trump! Vote Pence!
We'll take us there.
Yes, Donald Trump.
He'll take us there.

It's his promise
To take us there.
America's promise, oh yes.
Trump will take us there.

It's Donald Trump
Who'll lead the way.
And I will help him,
If you'll clearly say.

(Soft audience chorus - mainly men, the
lines continuously repeated - begins
and underlies throughout following:)
   (Yes! The choice is so clear.
   Trump! Vote for Trump. Vote for
   Pence.)

America's done more good
Than any other nation.
We don't see darkness,
We see righteous elation.

America deserves gratitude,
Not Socialist discord.
America will be great again.
Trump has given us his word.

He'll take us there.
Trump will take us there!

It's Donald Trump
Who'll lead the way.
And I will help him,
If you'll clearly say.

Donald Trump is no debater.
He is a forceful doer.
He states his mind, yes,
He's no apologetic mewler.

We need inspiration,
Not Socialism's discord.
We need our Founders' freedoms,
And he has pledged his word
To take us there.
Trump will take us there.

It's Donald Trump
Who'll lead the way.
And I will help him,
If you'll clearly say.

He'll take us there.
Trump will take us there!
Help us. Help us.
We'll take you there.

(Chorus silent. Bass beat becomes
lighter, more sprightly, but still
gospel.)

PENCE (WITH AUDIENCE RESPONSE)
"SO, ARE YOU READY?"

So, are you ready?
Are you ready
To vote for Trump and Pence?
Say that you are ready
To vote for Trump and Pence.
Say you're ready, now,
To vote for us.
Come on, vote for Trump, yes,
Trump and Pence.

No street rioting
Will be tolerated.
(We'll vote for you.)
Law and order
Won't be debated.
(We'll vote for you.)

The Lord is the One
We put our faith in.
He is the perfecter of
This great nation.

So, are you ready?
(We'll vote for you.)
Is everybody ready?
(We'll vote for you.)
To vote for Trump and Pence?
(We'll vote for you.)
Then, come on, vote for Trump.
(We'll vote for you.)

Prosperity is the aim of
This administration.
Freedom is the source of
Our inspiration.

So, come on, vote for Trump.
(We'll vote with you.)
Yes, come on, vote for Pence.
(We'll vote for you.)
Trump, yes! And Pence!
(We'll vote with you.)
Trump! And Pence!
(We'll vote for you.)
(Repeat and fade.)

BLACKOUT.

LIGHTS UP ON SOUTH LAWN OF WHITE HOUSE.
EVENING, WITH PORTICO PILLARS BRIGHTLY LIT.
STAGE RIGHT: TRUMP AT LECTERN, FACING OUT.
STANDING ARE VICE PRESIDENT AND KAREN PENCE,
MELANIA AND A EXCEEDINGLY TALL YOUNG BARRON
TO HIS LEFT. THE LATTER ALL SIT AS TRUMP
ACKNOWLEDGES THE APPLAUSE.

TRUMP
Thank you very much. Thank you very much.
Thank you very much.... I stand before you
tonight honored by your support, proud of
the extraordinary progress we have made
together over the last four incredible years
and blooming with confidence in the bright
future we will build for America in the next
four years.

LECTERN AND TRUMP BEGIN TO RISE SLOWLY.

This election will decide if we allow a
Socialist agenda to demolish our cherished
destiny, if we give free rein to violent

anarchists and agitators and criminals. Joe
Biden will be the destroyer of America's
greatness. He has spent his entire career on
the wrong side of history. Everything we
have achieved is now in danger. I cannot
watch this betrayal of our country any
longer. America first!

DOWNLIGHT ON TRUMP'S HAIR BRIGHTENS.

(TRUMP leans onto lectern.)

Joe Biden doesn't have a clue. If he got
elected, America would suffer a painful
shutdown. His four trillion dollar tax hike
would collapse our economy. China would own
America. With that far Left senator, crazy
Bernie Sanders, at his back, he's a Trojan
horse for godless Socialism.

Their manifesto calls for releasing nearly
half a million criminals onto the streets
and into your neighborhoods. We must never
allow mob rule. We can never allow mob rule.
We must always have law and order!

TRUMP AND LECTERN HAVE RISEN TO MAXIMUM
EXTENT.

(TRUMP looks down over the assembly.)

Together, we will write the next chapter of
the great American story. We will make
America safer, stronger, prouder, greater
than ever.

So tonight, I say to all Americans, this is
the most important election in the history
of our country.

(Much applause, which fades slowly.)

MAN PEEKS OUT FROM FAR STAGE LEFT. HE IS
HIGHLIGHTED AS LIGHTS DIM.

(MAN slowly nods affirmatively.)

BLACKOUT.

LIGHTS UP ON MELLON AUDITORIUM, AS BEFORE.
LECTERN IS LIT BUT UNOCCUPIED. THE VERY
LARGE MONITOR SCREEN AT REAR STAGE RIGHT
BRIGHTENS. SENATOR MCCONNELL APPEARS, WITH
BUCOLIC KENTUCKY LANDSCAPE IN BACKGROUND.

    (McCONNELL shifts slowly side to side
    as he speaks.)

                MCCONNELL
It's an honor to come before you tonight
from the Commonwealth of Kentucky. President
Trump knows he's inherited the first
generation of Americans who couldn't promise
their children a better life than their own.
Today's Democrat party doesn't want to
improve life. They want to decide how we
should live our lives. They want ... They
want ... They want ...

    (A sleek thoroughbred HORSE starts
    cross the field behind McCONNELL's
    image.)

                MCCONNEL
They want ... They want ... They want ...

    (As he speaks, HORSE lifts tail as it
    passes out of view.)

                MCCONNELL
Now you understand why Democrats tell us
about who Joe Biden is, not what he intends
to do.

    (McCONNELL's eyes flick to one side,
    in direction of departing HORSE.)

Reelect my friend, President Donald Trump.

<u>MCCONNELL'S IMAGE FADES. MONITOR GOES DARK.</u>

<u>FLASH. GIULIANI SUDDENLY AT LECTERN, IN
SOMBER SUIT AND WITH STARK BLACK, HEAVY
FRAME GLASSES.</u>

GIULIANI

My name is Rudy Giuliani. I'm the former
mayor of New York City. Well, my friends,
either you're not paying attention to recent
events or you don't think you'll be affected
by riots and anarchy in our downtown
streets. Let me tell you.

GIULIANI
"TROUBLE"

(Rhythmic speech)
*New York had that trouble, my friends,
after I was mayor.*
*Trouble, I say, right there in New York
City.*
Why sure I was tough mayor,
As I'm mighty proud to say.
Always proud to be called that.
*I consider the effort I made in New
York,*
To turn it into America's safest city,
*Is something anyone would be proud to
say.*
It took a cool head and lots of work
To not give in to the liberals
*Who wanted to expand their progressive
ways.*
*See what's happening in Democrat cities
right now?*
*Turning peaceful protests into vicious,
brutal riots.*

Disorder, looting, and violent crime!
It's what happened in New York after I
was mayor,
After the Leftist crazies took over
Gracie Mansion.

But, as I said,
It takes leadership and a disciplined
work ethic
To control a big city, or a big
country.
Any fool could just let it go
And let the Leftists have their way.
They'd call that "progress,"
But it's the first big step on the road
To anarchy and to revolution.
Look here. First it's let them out of
jail.
Then it's saying stealing what you need
isn't a crime.
And before you know
People are climbing in through your
windows,
Dressed in black with flashlights in
their hands,
To take what they like because some
politico
Says taking is okay if they need it.
Not bothering to go earn, no,
Just saying that it being what you want
is enough.

Friends, do you want to have everything you own
Up for grabs by anyone who won't be bothered to get a job?
Well, I should say not!
Friends, here's what I mean:
There are riots, fires, looting in our cities,
Trouble that marks the difference
Between a protestor and a vandal,
Vandal, with a capital "V"
And that rhymes with "B"
And that stands for "Biden."

Friends, with Biden in the White House
The Anarchists will be in charge.
I say, the Anarchists will run the show,
Taking your money to further Socialism.
To tax and spend. Spend and tax!
Never mind that you earned what you have,
That you want to keep what you've worked for,
That you want your home and family to be safe.
Never mind that not wanting to work
Is no reason to be taken care of by the state,
To be free to do drugs and get into trouble.
Yes, to make lots and lots of trouble.

*Just imagine the damage Socialism will
do
If Democrats ever get control of this
country!
Radical Liberalism throughout the land.
And that means trouble.
Trouble is what you'll get from Kamala.
Kamala, with a capital "K"
And that rhymes with "J"
And that stand for "Joe."*

*Friends, Russia had its Joe and we saw
how that turned out.
Not here. No, Siree. Not with Donald
Trump in charge.
I know you see through the Democrats.
You've heard and read what they have to
say,
That the government knows better than
the people.
The Democrats have our President to
beat
And a country to destroy,
So they pump up their media shills to
lie.
They pound you with their radical
agenda
To trick you into putting Biden and
Harris in charge,
Who'll bring lawlessness to our cities.
They want to handcuff the police,
So that four-year-olds can be murdered
And high schoolers killed when on their
way*

To play basketball with their friends!
Pro-criminal, anti-police, Socialist
policies
Put out by defective candidates of the
Left
Who threaten your daughters and your
sons.

That's trouble, friends.
That's the way of the jungle:
Anarchy and lawlessness.
But law and order shouldn't be for
sale.
And narchy shouldn't be a political
platform. No.
Friends, give our President four more
years.
Else there's much trouble, so much
trouble
Heading into our capitol city,
Trouble with a capital "T"
And that rhymes with "B"
And that stands for Biden.

(Normal speech)

Friends, in critical times in our history,
America has always been blessed with the
right person. Mister President, make our
nation safe!

SLOW FADE ON LECTERN.

BLACKOUT.

LIGHTS UP ON NETWORK CONVENTION COVERAGE.
CNN READERS ONE AND TWO AT DESK STAGE RIGHT.

FOX READER ONE
Well, President Trump's speech ran long, but
was one of the best speeches of his
political career.

FOX READER TWO
He made his case. Although, in many ways, it
wasn't much different from the Democrats'
theater of last week. Wouldn't you say?

FOX READER ONE
Oh, much more substance. He did a much
better job of contrasting his and Biden's
visions. Still, as with the Democrats and
their convention, the outcome wasn't in
doubt.

FOX READER TWO
No, it wasn't. You'd have to say that this
was a Trump Convention more than a
Republican Convention. George Bush didn't
even make a cameo appearance.

FOX READER ONE
That's true. And Senator Graham didn't
either. That surprised me. He's been a
loyal, outspoken supporter.

FOX READER TWO
Perhaps that's why he didn't need him.
Besides, Donald Trump prefers being his own
spokesperson. He's probably right to do so,
especially when it comes to appealing to his
base. His methods are quite clear.

FOX READER ONE
And effective.

FOX READERS DUET
"THERE HE GOES AGAIN"

Well, there he goes again,
Engaging his fond supporters.
Who are we to say that's wrong.
It makes good sense for him to focus
On those who love him.

They find his words so stirring and so
strong,
Aren't concerned with facts.

Prone to orate, he speaks to eager
ears,
Knows their thoughts control what they
hear,
Keeps alive their fears
Of what may come,
Of what had come,
Of what may come.

This election is the time for bold
saying,
To expose the tricks voters know the
Left is playing.
Democrats, they have lied and hoaxed
too long.
Trump's base is tired of their radical
song.

Trump appeared nearly every night.
Each session was themed and ambitious.
It was four proud days of celebration.

The words this Thursday night
Focused on America, This Land of
Greatness,
And on the history of a unique nation,
And of four more years.

Like a drum beat, it was pounded home.
Anxiety linked to what they've shown,
To what they've known,
To what they fear,
To what he says,
To what they fear.

Facts don't matter to many, that's been
made clear.
The only things that matter are what
they do hear.
Politicians come and politicians go.
Their power comes from shaping what
voters know.

Yes, Trump's made his points again.
That's fine. They need to hear them.
Nothing wrong in preaching to the
choir.
Those who watched at home
Saw an event that was quite thrilling.
He made good use of his White House
hour.
Four more years!

Like a drum beat, he pounded it home.
Anxiety linked to what he's shown,
To what they've known,

To wi ⌐ they fear,
To what he says,
To what they fear.

FOX READER ONE

Yes, another term for Donald Trump. There was some talk of a surprise for the VP slot, but nothing was going to come from that.

FOX READER TWO

No. Pence is perfect for President Trump. Loyal and supportive, almost to a fault.

FOX READER ONE

You think he's going to run — Pence is going to run, I mean — in 2024?

FOX READER TWO

Oh, absolutely. He's doing everything he can to pave that path. But that's step two. Right? At this point in his political career his strategy is to get those important next four years for Trump.

FOX READER ONE

I agree. He needs to highlight the Democrats' mistakes and point out how their platform reeks of Socialist overreach.

FOX READER TWO

In some ways that's easy. Trump's base doesn't need convincing. They love him, and hate the Left. The bigger question is how that will play out elsewhere.

FOX READER ONE

I have to add: Why they had Giuliani close yet didn't let Graham say a word was a puzzle.

FOX READER TWO

Perhaps President Trump was thinking about how Graham characterized him early in 2016.

FOX READER ONE

Ouch!

LIGHTING SHIFTS TO FAVOR CNN DESK.

CNN READER ONE

Another long one from Trump. Almost as long
as Clinton's — Bill's, I mean. Remember
that?

CNN READER TWO

Oh, I remember. About seventy minutes, this
one was. Trump loves being on stage as much
as Clinton.

CNN READER ONE

And he loves attacking. Attack and attack,
people and ideas. The President's aim was
clear tonight: Blame the Democrats for
anything bad he can dig out and warn of what
they'll do wrong in the future. It doesn't
seem to trouble him to exaggerate.

CNN READER TWO

Even to the point of mischaracterization.
Like I said, he loves being on stage. The
late night folks will lose a lot of good
copy if he isn't reelected.

CNN READER ONE

It'll be worth it.

CNN READERS DUET
"WELL, THERE THEY ARE AGAIN"

Well, there they are again,

The old, disproven stories.

*You'd think that he'd give up that
chase.*

But it worked for him the last time.

No surprise he won't change them now.

Facts don't seem to matter to his base.

They love him even more.

Like a drummer, he pounded it home,
Stoking anger at what they're shown,
At what they have known,
At what had come,
At what is now,
At what may come.

Facts don't matter to many, that's been
made clear.
The only things that matter are what
they do hear.
Politicians come and politicians go.
Their power comes from shaping what
voters know.

Too bad we're just repeating
These same, old observations.
But the patterns are so starkly clear.
It's sad to see dark chapters
of our past reopened
And drawing grim history far too near,
Lies obscuring deep truths.

Like a drummer, he pounds it home,
Links their fears to what can't be
shown.
Happy that what they want
Is what he wants to say,
Is what they think,
Is what he wants to say.

Facts don't matter to many, that's been
made clear.
The only things that matter are what
they do hear.
Politicians come and politicians go.
Their power comes from shaping what
voters know.

Yes, there they are again,
Ghosts of deep state visions.
Trump knows that they strike minor
chords.
He doesn't need
Conspiracies that actually are real.
It's sufficient that he's fluent with
angry words.
That's served him well.

Like a drummer, he pounds it home,
Links their fears to what can't be
shown.
Happy that what they want
Is what he wants to say,
Is what they think,
Is what he wants to say.

CNN READER ONE
He's going to need help from the middle,
from the undecided more than in twenty
sixteen. If he just did that one thing
everyone's been talking about. If he would
clearly denounce the white supremacists, it
would help him with the moderates.

CNN READER TWO

Perhaps he doesn't care about them, the
moderates. He certainly seems to spend the
most effort on solidifying and gratifying
his core people.

CNN READER ONE

That's easy. But will that be enough? Are
there enough votes there for him?

CNN READER TWO

In some states sure. But overall? I doubt
it. I think he feels whatever votes he might
lose will be outweighed by those he gains.
Note that I said "feels" not "calculates."
It would be interesting to know how much of
what we see is his reelection team's
strategy and how much is just Trump. He
wants love, from whomever, and doesn't seem
to care about criticism.

CNN READER ONE

Exactly. He just dismisses that as more fake
media lies from that imaginary "deep state."

CNN READER TWO

I was surprised, though, by Trump's strong
support for that Marjorie Greene in Georgia,
even after all the criticism for his failure
to denounce white supremacists. Really, who
takes that QAnon fairytale seriously?

CNN READER ONE

Quite a few it seems. And can you believe
that Giuliani? (Chuckles) The perfect legal
mind for Trump!

CNN READER TWO

Yes. Giuliani gets a prime spot and Senator
Graham doesn't even get to show up at all.
Lindsey's been one of his biggest boosters
the past several years.

CNN READER ONE

Maybe the Trump campaign was afraid he might give an honest assessment, like he did in 2016.

CNN READER TWO

No fear of anything honest from Lindsey Graham now, any more than from Rudy, ever!

FOX AND CNN DESKS EVENLY LIT.

READERS QUARTET
(CONTINUATION OF ABOVE)

Like a drummer, he pounds it home,
Links their fears to what can't be
shown.
Happy that what they want
Is what he wants to say,
Is what they think,
Is what he wants to say.

Facts don't matter to many, that's been
made clear.
The only things that matter are what
they do hear.
Politicians come and politicians go.
Their power comes from shaping what
voters know.

> (CNN READERS ONE and TWO look to one side, take off their lapel mics. CNN READER ONE looks to READER TWO and laughs aloud.)

CNN READERS DUET
"POLITICS IS STRANGE"

Politics,
Politics is strange.
\

Most people
Take it for a game.

Once you're in it,
It becomes a compulsive mix.
The people whom you need aren't
Always those you get to pick.

The average voter
Would prefer to choose.
But a politician,
If he did that he would lose.

So politicians
Accept a varied lot.
When they are campaigning
It's the only chance they've got.

(Music continues as CNN READERS mouth
words. Music pauses.)

CNN READER ONE
(Turning to his partner.) Tell me.

CNN READER TWO
What can I tell you?

CNN READER ONE
What promises should politicians make?

CNN READER TWO
Whatever seems to work.

CNN READER ONE
And if they don't work?

CNN READER TWO
Then they must say them louder.

                              CNN READER ONE
And if they still don't work?

                              CNN READER TWO
Simply say:

   Voters, my dear voters,
   My opponents think you're fools.

   Voters, worried voters,
   I must win to make new rules.

   Voters, my dear voters,
   My opponents always lie.
   Voter, oh my voters,
   If I lose you can kiss you hopes
   goodbye.

                              CNN READERS DUET
   Voters, dear voters,
   The opponents think you're fools.
   Voters, worried voters,
   Our side must win to make new rules.

   Voters, oh dear voters,
   The opponents always lie.
   Voters, oh anxious voters,
   If they win you can kiss you hopes
   goodbye.

          (Joint laughter.)

LIGHTING SLOWLY DIMS.

BLACKOUT

                      END OF ACT TWO

ACT THREE

LIGHTS UP ON OVAL OFFICE. TRUMP TALKING WITH
MARK MEADOWS AND BILL BARR

TRUMP
Have you read any of this garbage, Mark?
Bill? This Woodward's "Rage" fiction? He
sent me a copy. (Sarcastic) Such a nice guy.

(TRUMP throws book into waste
basket.)

Don't waste your time. Hoax. Total, total
hoax. All made up. A bunch of made-up quotes
and misquotes. Just like Bolton's and
Cohen's crap. Lies, just to make a few
dollars. At least they signed their crap,
not like that coward who hid for years
before he owned up his trash. "Anonymous,"
he called himself. Wasn't that it, Bill?

BARR
Taylor, Sir. Miles Taylor. Yes, and very
unfair.

MEADOWS
A monumental embarrassment and about as
exciting as a Scooby-Doo episode. Another
low-level, disgruntled former staffer
trying, like you said, Mister President, to
make a few bucks for himself.

TRUMP
Good thing my people don't read books. You
should have kept their garbage — Cohen's and
Bolton's, at least — from being published in

- 125 -

the first place. A pair of disgruntled losers who were lousy at their jobs. There were quite a few others that[sic] were mistakes. Big, big mistakes, some of them. Didn't get rid of them fast enough.

VOICE OF MAN
(In background, diffusely and slowly reading off names ad lib during below:) Comey. Scaramiucci. Bannon. Omarosa. McCabe. McMaster. Tillerson. Kelly. Cohen. McGahn. Sessions.

TRUMP
I should have gotten rid of Bolton even sooner. You know that. Everyone knows that.

BARR AND MEADOWS
Yes, Sir.

TRUMP
It's very, very sad how these bad people, once you get rid of them, they can come out with these made-up books, just to get media time. Very sad. I wonder if we'll see one from Vindman. I suppose so. He's another (scrathes air-quotes) "big thoughts" guy. His brother has even less to say, but he'll probably jump on the wagon, too. It's what losers like them do. A way to get a little money and a few minutes of fame.

TRUMP
"A DISGRUNTLED BUNCH, ONE AND ALL"
It doesn't matter what staff thinks,
As long as it's kept under lock and key.
I need people who will go along
And steadfastly agree with me.

I gave many their chance to shine.
But when I found out they weren't good,
I didn't waste time with playing games,
Got rid of them fast as I could.

A disgruntled bunch, one and all.
A disgruntled bunch, one and all.
One by one they're gone.
The disgruntled ones gone,
Pushed right out the door.
And, I am not through.
Any whiner will be shown the door!

Those who weren't good at their jobs
I enjoyed letting them go.
No, no one likes being fired.
You could see that on my show.
It's sad when those who are given a
chance,
To show what they could do,
Instead go rogue and put out lies,
Their incompetence coming through.

BARR AND MEADOWS
A disgruntled bunch, one and all.
A disgruntled bunch, one and all.
One by one they're gone.
The disgruntled ones gone,
Fired or pushed out the door.
And, he is not through.
All the losers will be shown the door!

TRUMP

*Some weren't honest in taking up their
tasks.
They were here but not willing to play.
They hid in the weeds, nursing their
needs.
So why should they get to stay?
Others you could tell from the very
first day
Were simply not up to the heat.
Instead of admitting they were out of
their league,
They took their complaints to the
street.*

BARR AND MEADOWS

*A disgruntled bunch, one and all.
A disgruntled bunch, one and all.
One by one they've gone
The disgruntled ones gone,
Fired or pushed out the door.
And, he is not through.
All the losers will be shown the door!*

TRUMP

*Bolton was one, Tillerson too.
Lightweights who disregarded the plan.
Their pasts were no reason to stay on
the job.
Best to discard such as quick as you
can.
The books they wrote are full of lies.
They said whatever it took for a buck.*

I gave them a chance to step up and shine.
Instead they put out pure muck.

Send them packing, one and all.
Get rid of them, one and all.
An incompetent gone, a disgruntled one gone.
All best out the door.
And, I am not through.
More will soon be shown the door.

Mattis, as I proved right, was an overrated guy.
A bad, bad leader and in the ISIS fight
He came across as much too shy.
I need people who are loyal to me,
People who know up is the way to go.
When an anti-Trumper is finally unmasked
It was time for them to be off the show.

TRUMP (WITH BARR AND MEADOWS)
Yes. Yes. Yes.
A disgruntled bunch, one and all.
A disgruntled bunch, one and all.
One by one they're gone,
The disgruntled ones gone,
Fired or pushed out the door.
And, I am (he is) not through.
All the losers will be soon shown the door!

VOICE OF MAN
(As above:) Mattis. Bolton. Volker. Spencer.

TRUMP
What about those people at Justice jumping
ship, Bill? Was it because of doing the
right thing for Roger Stone? Just because of
that?

BARR
No. Long time malcontents, as you said, Sir.
That was the lame excuse they put out there
—

TRUMP
Very, very lame.

BARR
... Democratic hold-overs trying to make a
political thing out of it and get
predictable media coverage for themselves.
Grandstanding.

VOICE OF MAN
(As above, gradually fading:) Sondland.
Mulvaney. Troye.

BLACKOUT.

AT REAR LIGHTS UP, TWO LARGE MONITORS HIGH
ON BACK WALL BEHIND STAGE. CNN LOGOED DESK
WITH TWO COMMENTATORS SHOWN ON ONE, STAGE
RIGHT. TWO FOX COMMENTATORS ON THE STAGE
LEFT MONITOR, SIMILARLY SET UP.

AT STAGE LIGHTS UP, THE FIRST PRESIDENTIAL
DEBATE AT CASE WESTERN RESERVE. BIDEN (STAGE
LEFT) AND TRUMP (STAGE RIGHT) AT SEPARATE
LECTERNS. LINGERING APPLAUSE FROM THEIR
ENTRY.

MODERATOR (**CHRIS WALLACE**) STAGE FRONT, AT
DESK, WITH BACK TO AUDIENCE.

(COMMENTATORS, otherwise immobile,
look down and follow the debate.)

<u>WALLACE'S FEW LINES ARE SPOKEN CLEARLY. THE
TWO CANDIDATES PROVIDE SNATCHES OF SEMANTIC
SPEECH BUT THEIR DIALOGUE IS MAINLY
ASEMANTIC, I.E., WALLA AND GIBBERISH, E.G.,
AD LIB "RHUBARB RHUBARB," "MURMUR MURMUR,"
"BOOGLE BOGLE," "THE CLICK ROUND FLOCKS
THUMPS AND CRAZY SOCKS," ETC, ETC. TRUMP'S
TONAL PATTERN IS COMBATIVE, TERSE, QUERULOUS
THROUGHOUT. BIDEN, INITIALLY CALM AND
EXPANSIVE, GRADUALLY TAKES ON A TONE OF
IRRITATION AND IS OCCASIONALLY DISJOINTED.</u>

(BIDEN gives a "fists up" gesture to
the audience and to WALLACE from his
lectern.)

WALLACE
Gentlemen, a lot of people have been waiting
for this night. So let's get going. Our
first subject is the Supreme Court....
President Trump, in the first segment you go
first. Two minutes.

TRUMP
Walla walla elections have consequences.
Walla walla.

WALLACE
Mister Vice President.

BIDEN
(After coughing into his hand.) We're in an
election already. Walla walla. I am the
Democratic party right now. Walla walla.

TRUMP
(Shaking head and interrupting above.) Walla
walla. (Accusative, over BIDEN.) Walla walla
military people walla walla. Walla walla
China walla walla.

- 131 -

WALLACE

Mister President. Mister President. Mister President. I am the moderator. (To Biden) Go ahead.

BIDEN

Walla walla.

TRUMP

(Over BIDEN.) Walla walla.

WALLACE

Mister President.

TRUMP

(Over BIDEN and WALLACE) Walla walla.

WALLACE

Mister President.

TRUMP

Walla walla.

WALLACE

Mister President. I am the moderator today, and I'd like you to let me ask my question.

TRUMP

Walla walla health care walla walla.

BIDEN

Walla walla. Everybody knows he's a liar. Walla walla.

TRUMP

(Constantly interrupting) Walla walla, walla walla!

BIDEN

Walla walla take coverage away walla walla.

TRUMP
(Interrupting) Walla walla China plague
walla walla (combative) Obama care, it's a
disaster walla walla.

WALLACE
Please let the Vice President respond.

BIDEN
Walla walla doesn't know what he's talking
about. Here's the thing walla walla.

WALLACE
Let's go on. Mister Vice President, are you
going to tell the American people tonight
whether or not you are going to support
packing the Supreme Court?

BIDEN
I'll take a position when that becomes an
issue.

TRUMP
Answer the question.

BIDEN
The people should vote. Vote walla walla.

TRUMP
(Confounding BIDEN's attempt to speak.) Why
won't you answer the question? Why walla
walla?

BIDEN
(Testy) Will you shut up, man?

WALLACE
Gentlemen, let's go on to the next segment.

(Debate participants freeze.)

MONITORS AT STAGE REAR BRIGHTEN.

CNN COMMENTATOR ONE
This is getting hard to watch. It's not a
debate.

CNN COMMENTATOR TWO
No. It's more like a cage fight.

FOX COMMENTATOR ONE
The President as racking Biden over the
coals.

FOX COMMENTATOR TWO
This is almost fun. The poor old guy can't
even get his sentences together.

(Debate resumes, participants thaw.)

WALLACE
The question is why should America trust you
more than your opponent? (To BIDEN) You
first, Sir. Two minutes uninterrupted.

BIDEN
Good luck. Walla walla COVID walla walla. It
is what it is, he said. Walla walla.

TRUMP
(Interrupting BIDEN, to WALLACE) He walla
walla. (To BIDEN) You don't know walla walla
you don't know walla walla. (To WALLACE)
Just a minute ... Just a minute.

BIDEN
Look, walla walla masks walla walla smart
walla walla, for the sake of all Americans.

TRUMP
Don't use the word smart with me! Walla
walla shutdown?! Walla walla cripple the
greatest economy we've ever seen. Walla
walla biggest mask you've ever seen.

BIDEN
Walla walla. (To TRUMP) You're the worst
President we've ever had. C'mon, walla
walla.

TRUMP
(Over BIDEN) In forty-seven months I've done
more than you have in forty-seven years.
Walla walla, Chris, Chris, walla walla.

WALLACE
(Trying to regain some semblance of control)
Mister President. Mister President. Your
campaign agreed to the format. Please let —
Please let Vice President Biden have his two
minutes then you can respond.

TRUMP AND BIDEN
(Discordant) Walla walla, walla walla!

(Debate trio freezes.)

(On monitors, each COMMENTATOR looks
to their partner. FOX COMMENTATORS
smile. CNN COMMENTATORS examine their
watches.)

(Debate resumes.)

WALLACE
(Calmly) Two minutes uninterrupted. Why
should Black Americans trust you over your
opponent? Mister Vice President, you go
first.

BIDEN
Walla walla torches walla walla bile walla
walla there were "very fine people on both
sides," he said walla walla. He's a racist.

TRUMP
(Interrupting) You called them super
predators. Walla walla radical Democrats

walla walla law and order walla walla. Look
what happened. Look at Chicago walla walla.

WALLACE
Excuse me sir.

TRUMP
(Speaking over Wallace) Walla walla.

WALLACE
(To TRUMP) I'm asking —

TRUMP
(Speaking over Wallace) Walla walla.

WALLACE
I'm asking — I'm asking — Would you like to
switch seats?

TRUMP
Walla walla!

WALLACE
Mister President, are you willing, tonight,
to condemn white supremacists?

TRUMP
Give me a name. Give me a name walla walla.
Proud boys? Proud Boys, stand down and stand
by. Walla walla problem is the Left walla
walla antifa walla walla radical,
revolutionary sensitivity training walla
walla.

BIDEN
His own FBI director walla walla.

TRUMP AND BIDEN
Walla walla! Walla walla!

WALLACE
We're done. Let's move on to the next
question.

TRUMP
(Persisting) Walla walla greatest economy
walla walla COVID walla walla the VA a mess
under him.

(Debate participants freeze for a
moment.)

WALLACE
(Resuming) Why should the voters elect you
president over your opponent? Two minutes,
uninterrupted, Mister Vice President.

BIDEN
Walla walla ... walla walla ... walla walla.

TRUMP
Walla walla, walla walla, walla walla!

WALLACE
Mister President. Mister President.

TRUMP
(Over Biden and Wallace.) No president has
done more than I. None. Walla walla the
greatest walla walla.

WALLACE
Mister President. Your campaign agreed ...
Your campaign agreed to these rules. Why
can't you abide by that agreement?

BIDEN
Walla walla.

TRUMP
(Interrupting) Walla walla forty-seven years
walla walla.

TRUMP AND BIDEN
Walla walla! Walla walla.

WALLACE
Gentlemen. Gentlemen. The final segment ...

BIDEN
Let people vote. Vote. Vote. Vote.

TRUMP
Walla walla coup walla walla caught them all
walla walla. It'll be a fraud walla walla
fraudulent election walla walla dumped in
rivers walla walla unrequested ballots.

BIDEN
This man has no idea what he's taking about.
Walla walla. Here's the deal ...

BIDEN AND TRUMP
Walla walla. Walla walla, walla walla!

WALLACE
Excuse me. (Waving hands, having lost
control) Excuse me. I have a final question.
I have — I have — I hope neither of you will
interrupt the other. The final question:
Will you not declare victory until the
election is certified? President Trump you
go first.

TRUMP
Walla walla bad things in Philadelphia walla
walla they cheat, they cheat. Walla walla
fraudulent walla walla!

WALLACE
Okay — Fine — Vice President Biden.

TRUMP
(Over others) Walla walla lost ballots walla
walla destroyed walla walla.

WALLACE
Vice President Biden. Same final question to
you.

                         BIDEN
Yes. Here's the deal. (Struggling to
overcome TRUMP's serial interruptions) Walla
walla it's honest.

                         TRUMP
(Over others) Walla walla, walla walla.
Walla walla. Walla walla!

                        WALLACE
Please, Mister President. Vice President
Biden, go ahead.

                         BIDEN
He has no idea what he's talking about.
Walla walla, walla walla.

                         TRUMP
(Over BIDEN) Walla walla, walla walla!

                        WALLACE
Gentlemen, that's the end of it. This's the
end of this debate. We're going to leave it
there. It's been an interesting hour and a
half.

           (Debate trio goes static.)

LECTERN LIGHTING DIMS. MONITORS BEHIND
BRIGHTEN.

  CNN COMMENTATOR ONE AND FOX COMMENTATOR ONE
(Looking to their respective partner.) Chris
Wallace certainly has that correct. It has
been interesting.

                CNN COMMENTATOR TWO
It was horrific. A disgrace. I can't imagine
who won.

                CNN COMMENTATOR ONE
It was like a cage fight. No rules. How can
you say who won?

CNN COMMENTATOR TWO
I agree. It was not a debate. It was a brawl. How can you say who won?

CNN COMMENTSTOR ONE
Depends on your biases, I suppose.

CNN COMMENTATOR TWO
What IS clear is that America lost tonight.

FOX COMMENTATOR TWO
(Big smile) Biden was steamrolled. He was simply steamrolled by the President. He couldn't keep up.

FOX COMMENTATOR ONE
Yes. He came off as frustrated and cranky, like he needed his nap.

FOX COMMENTATOR TWO
He seemed to be struggling at times. Painful to watch, (big smile) if you're a Democrat.

FOX COMMENTATOR ONE
Overall, Biden was very weak tonight, as usual.

FOX COMMENTATOR TWO
You'd have to say Biden simply was beat up. It was a SmackDown.

FOX COMMENTATOR ONE
That's good. That's good. Beat up and smacked down! It was all President Trump tonight.

FOX COMMENTATORS DUET
"BEAT UP, SMACKED DOWN IN THE DEBATE TODAY."
They watched in their city,
They watched sitting in their home
town.

As Trump beat up on Sleepy Joe.
They watched as Biden got smacked down.

You could count on Biden
To mouth his Socialist cant.
He tried to make his a reasoned plan,
But in truth all he could do is rant.
Beat up, smacked down in the debate
today.

Beat up, smacked down in the debate
today.
Beat up, smacked down in the debate
today.
Beat up, smacked down in the debate
today.
Biden was the loser in the debate
today!

The President crafted careful argument.
In contrast, Biden simply came off
weak.
While Trump spoke with strong
sentiment,
Joe stuttered and sometimes found it
hard to speak.

Beat up, smacked down in the debate
today.
Beat up, smacked down in the debate
today.
Beat up, smacked down in the debate
today.

Biden was the loser in the debate
today!

While we watched this first debate
unfold,
Sleepy Joe found it increasingly hard
to talk.
His weak smiles were of someone sadly
old.
He was picked to run but showed he can
barely walk.

Beat up, smacked down in the debate
today.
Beat up, smacked down in the debate
today.
Beat up, smacked down in the debate
today.
Biden was the loser in the debate
today!

The Democrats, they've given up the
fight
And are helping us win by running Joe
Biden.
Watching him squirm up there tonight,
You could see him searching, searching
for a hole to hide in.

Vice Presidential debate is coming soon
And we'll watch Pence as he deflates
Harris.

It'll the same result in a different
room.
Her radical Socialist ideas will be
easy to embarrass.
But Biden was the loser in the debate
today!

Beat up, smacked down in the debate
today.
Beat up, smacked down in the debate
today.
Beat up, smacked down in the debate
today.
Biden was the loser in the debate
today!

Trump shot Joe down with both barrels,
Calling out the China deals of his
thieving son,
And the father's decades of doing
nothing.
Watching Joe look down was almost fun.

Disastrous health care plan was yet one
more
Of the burdens the Democrats had laid
on American's backs.
There was the lost jobs, the endless
war,
Biden's sick VA, and his racist jailing
of "predator blacks."
Beat up, smacked down in the debate
today.

*Beat up, smacked down in the debate
today.*
*Beat up, smacked down in the debate
today.*
*Beat up, smacked down in the debate
today.*
*Biden was the loser in the debate
today!*

Yes, yes!

*Beat up, smacked down in the debate
today.*
*Beat up, smacked down in the debate
today.*
*Beat up, smacked down in the debate
today.*
*Biden was the loser in the debate
today!*

BLACKOUT.

SOUND OF HELICOPTER BUILDING IN BACKGROUND.

VOICE OF NEWSREADER
(Offstage) President Trump is being flown
today to the Walter Reed military hospital
in Bethesda, Maryland. The President, we
have been told, had become feverish and
fatigued shortly after his positive COVID
test. (Pause) There goes Marine One, taking
President Trump to Walter Reed. We and the
nation wish him well. After these many
months of ...

SOUND OF HELICOPTER DROWNS OUT NEWSREADER
THEN FADES.

LIGHTS BARELY UP ON A LARGE HOSPITAL ROOM.
IN DIM LIGHTING, THE SCREENS AND INDICATOR
LIGHTS OF NUMEROUS MEDICAL DEVICES DOMINATE
A FIGURE IN BED, TRUMP, COVERED WITH A GREEN
BLANKET. TWO DESKS AND SEVERAL CHAIRS ARE
OFF TO ONE SIDE.

>   (An oxygen mask over his face, TRUMP
>   stares upward.)

VOICE OF NEWSREADER
(Also offstage but distinct from previous)
It appears that a number of presidential
staff and aides have tested positive for the
Corona virus. The medical consensus is that
this is the result of the White House Rose
Garden receptions and the lack of
preventative measures at such large
gatherings. Here with her assessment is ...

VOICE FADES. ROOM LIGHTS BRIGHTEN.

>   (**HANDSOME DOCTOR,** in lab coat, enters
>   and stands next to bed.)

HANDSOME DOCTOR
Good evening, Mister President. How are you
feeling?

TRUMP
(Vague, indiscernible mumbling.)

HANDSOME DOCTOR
(Glances to one side.) The oximeter has been
showing steady high nineties. No more dips.
I think we can take the mask off now, at
least for a while. I know it's uncomfortable
for you.

>   (HANDSOME DOCTOR leans over bed and
>   removes mask from TRUMP's face.)

We'll keep the monitors in place, of course,
but you'll probably have a better sleep

- 145 -

without this. We've given you something to counter that fever, knock it down. Otherwise, I'm happy to say that everything looks good, Mister President. Nothing dramatic in the lungs.

                    TRUMP
I hate masks.... I need to make an appearance, make some kind of statement. The election is in just a few weeks. I need to show I've beaten this thing and feeling really good before debating Sleepy Joe.

                HANDSOME DOCTOR
Tomorrow would be a good time. In the meantime, I suggest you get a good night's sleep.

          (HANDSOME DOCTOR salutes the supine
          figure. TRUMP lifts one hand in
          response. HANDSOME DOCTOR leaves.)

ROOM LIGHTS DIM VERY SLOWLY AS FOUR NARROWLY DOWNLIT FIGURES APPEAR NEXT TO BED, TWO NEAR ITS FOOT, ONE IN THE MIDDLE, ONE AT THE HEAD. EACH IS ENVELOPED IN A LOOSE PPE GOWN.

          (TRUMP fidgets under blanket.)

BED FULLY LIT.

FIGURE FARTHEST FROM HEAD OF BED DROPS ITS GOWN, REVEALING A PALE AND MONOCHROME **CHUCK SCHUMER.**

                    SCHUMER
(With up-pointing flashlight under chin.) Greetings, Mister President. Feeling ill, is that it? I'm not surprised. The Democratic leadership is sick, you've said. Yet, it's YOU who's lying in bed here, paying the price. History will remember us both but you foremost, I dare say. And it won't be kind. In November we'll kick your 'effin ass and

we'll win. We'll win big. We'll even control
the Senate. (Voice fading) Control the
Senate. Control the Senate.

SCHUMER'S FLASHLIGHT AND DOWNLIGHT GO OFF.

ADJACENT FIGURE DROPS ITS GOWN, REVEALING A
FULL FIGURED, VERY PALE NANCY PELOSI IN A
TIGHT, STARKLY BRIGHT BLUE DRESS.

PELOSI
(With up-pointing flashlight under her
chin.) It's me, Crazy Nancy, Donald. The
third rate politician you find so
disgusting. But not so disgusting as the
child with doggy doo on his shoes I compared
you to. Yes, me, mentally disturbed but not
yet a psychopathic nut. How does it feel? To
be here alone? With no connection home? Like
a foolish clown? Yes, come November we'll
have the House and, if you're still in
office, we'll impeach you again. One way or
another, you'll soon be gone. We'll do it
again and you'll be gone (voice fading). Be
gone. Be gone.

PELOSI'S FLASHLIGHT AND DOWNLIGHT GO OFF.

ADJACENT FIGURE MOVES CLOSER TO BED, PUTS A
FLASHLIGHT UNDER ITS CHIN. IT'S A BLONDE,
VERY PALE **STORMY DANIELS**. SMILING, SHE DROPS
HER GOWN. NAKED, WITH HUGE, ALMOST
CARTOONISH BREASTS, SHE MOMENTARILY PLACES
THE FLASHLIGHT BELOW THEM THEN LOWERS IT
FURTHER.

DANIELS
(Flashlight again under her chin.) You
enjoyed it much more than I, didn't you?

(She puts a hand on TRUMP"s knee,
massaging it and stroking upwards.)

Cute little thing. With a big hat, like Toad in Mario Kart.

> (She puts her hand on TRUMP's crotch area, which begins to rise.)

We can have fun again. Would you like me to spank you? I can, even here. I still have that magazine.

> (She laughs as TRUMP's tumescence becomes extreme and raises the blanket further.)

You don't like coverings on your heads, big or small, do you, Donald? I didn't mind then and I don't mind now. But look at what not wearing a face mask has brought you ... COVID. (voice fading) COVID. COVID.

DANIELS' FLASHLIGHT AND DOWNLIGHT GO OFF.

> (TRUMP, head hard against the pillow, looks about, his tumescence still evident.)

FIGURE AT HEAD OF THE BED MOVES INTO TRUMP'S LINE OF SIGHT AND PUTS A FLASHLIGHT UNDER ITS CHIN. IT'S A VERY ROBUST LOOKING JOE BIDEN.

> (Trump's tumescence subsides.)

BIDEN
President Trump. You can't grab her (motioning) by the pussy now, can you? All hooked up and flat on your back. Sleepy Joe, you call me. Say I'm not alive. But it's you who doesn't look so good. This is the real deal, man. More than a PR problem, isn't it? I heard you don't like my ads and were pleased you didn't have to be nice anymore. Were you ever? I addressed you as President Trump but I should have used your full

title, Worst Possible President Trump. Get
well soon, clown. I want you to witness the
voters kicking you out, to know the feeling
of being fired. I want to see you laugh, if
you're able.

                    TRUMP
(Weakly) No. They love me. You can't beat
me. The voters, my base, they love me.

                    BIDEN
Maybe it won't be the voters who do you in,
clown. It will be the small things, the
little things, the things you can't fight
against or bully or shame. Things that can't
even be seen and are coursing through your
blood stream right now. Maybe you'll die
before you are fired.

                    TRUMP
No. I'm too strong. The strongest. They
can't. They won't. They love me.

                    BIDEN
You'll either die or be fired. (Voice
fading) Die or be fired, die or be fired.

          (BIDEN shines the flashlight in
          TRUMP's eyes.)

BIDEN'S DOWNLIGHT GOES OFF.

          (The other three visitors turn their
          flashlights on TRUMP's face and move
          the beams about. BIDEN puts his hand
          over TRUMP's nose and mouth. TRUMP
          struggles.)

ALL DOWNLIGHTS AND FLASHLIGHTS GO OFF. A
NURSE IS AT TRUMP'S BEDSIDE, REFITTING THE
OXYGEN MASK.

NURSE
Just for an hour or so, Mister President,
till the Doctor returns and can review the
oximeter data.

BLACKOUT

LIGHTS UP ON SPLIT STAGE, TWO DIFFERENT
VENUES. STAGE LEFT: BANK OF MICROPHONES IN
FRONT OF WALTER REED HOSPITAL STEPS.
HANDSOME DOCTOR AT MICROPHONE, AN ARRAY OF
MEDICAL COLLEAGUES BEHIND.

ELEVATED STAGE RIGHT: TRUMP ENTERS THEN,
DURING THE SPEECH BELOW, WALKS SLOWLY TO
MICROPHONE ON RAILED BALCONY AT WHITE HOUSE,
REMOVING HIS FACE MASK ENROUTE.

HANDSOME DOCTOR
(Multiple indistinct voices in background.)
No, I didn't, I cannot speak to that. We
felt it best not to go too deeply into the
President's medical condition at that time.
(Indistinct question in background.) Our
judgment was to be conservative. (Another
indistinct question in background.) Yes, we
felt three nights at Reed were sufficient.
He will have world class medical care at the
White House. (Another indistinct question.)
No, I cannot speak to that either, but he
hasn't presented fever for several days.

HANDSOME DOCTOR
"THE PRESIDENT'S WOKE"
Our President enjoys his lavish homes.
The one in D.C. is only one.
Because of the election he's been
forced to roam
And spend less time in Florida's
warming sun.

The current pandemic is rather grim.
The virus has laid so many low.
Trump's lucky to have staff stick with
him,
Despite Fauci's stern warnings of a
vicious foe.

Getting COVID was his gift from God.
Why just last week he'd called it a
joke.
Feeling it firsthand was an alerting
prod.
We can now rest easy, the President's
woke.

Thursday morning the President felt a
chill.
His head was achy and he felt quite
weak.
To prevent him from getting gravely ill
We decided to monitor him lest his
fever peak.

More tired the next day and rather hot,
Raising concerns that he'd find it hard
to breathe,
When his blood oxygen fell, though not
a lot,
We summoned Marine One to take him to
Reed.

Getting COVID was his gift from God.
Why just last week he'd called it a
joke.

*Feeling it firsthand was an alerting
prod.
We can now rest easy, the President's
woke.*

*His loyal base stood watch through
night and morn.
Inside, 'cept for medical staff, he was
quite alone.
When respiratory complaints raised more
concern,
We gave him remdesivir and
dexamethasone.*

*The President was anxious to greet his
base outside
And to resume his steady stream of
tweets.
So we allowed that he'd improved enough
for a ride,
As long as he returned to his critical
care suite.*

*Getting COVID was his gift from God.
Why just last week he'd called it a
joke.
Feeling it firsthand was an alerting
prod.
We can now rest easy, the President's
woke.*

*President Trump will go home today.
I believe that our work here is done.*

At the White House he'll be okay.
His chances of a relapse are next to
none.

He'll have comments to make, I'm sure,
About COVID and how it affected him.
The nation, the world is awaiting a
cure.
Meanwhile, like Trump, our team's
confident we'll win.

Getting COVID was his gift from God.
Why just last week he'd called it a
joke.
Feeling it firsthand was an alerting
prod.
We can now rest easy, the President's
woke.

TRUMP
(Hands on railing in front of him.) They
were great. A great, great team at Walter
Reed. Our Vets are lucky to have such people
to provide for them. As to my COVID, I'm
fine now. See? I beat it. It's no big deal.

TRUMP
"YOUR PRESIDENT'S WOKE"
(Continuing song.)
Don't let Fauci's scare talk get to
you.
Enjoy your lives and ignore dark fears.
It's not much worse than a case of the
flu.
I feel better now than I have in years.

*My Warp Speed team has earned your
ovation.*
COVID will be defeated by our vaccine.
*The Chinese plague that's infected our
nation*
*Will soon no longer be part of the
scene.*

Getting COVID was my gift from God.
Yes, just last week I said it's a joke.
*But feeling it firsthand was an
alerting prod.*
*You can now rest easy, your President's
woke.*

TRUMP (WITH HANDSOME DOCTOR)
*Getting COVID was my(his) gift from
God.*
*Yes, just last week I(he) called it a
joke.*
*Feeling it firsthand was an alerting
prod.*
*You can now rest easy, your President's
woke.*

TRUMP
Don't let all the scare talk dominate you.
I'm your leader. (Speaking faster and
faster.) I had to do this. I'm your leader.
I'm your leader.

> (TRUMP looks disoriented, stops,
> grasps railing, then taps it lightly.
> He turns and exits gingerly with a
> backward wave.)

BLACKOUT.

HANDSOME DOCTOR
Well, yes, agitation in some case, that's
true. Agitation, even paranoia on occasion.
But those are temporary side effects of
steroids, such as dexamathasone, and not a
concern in the President's case. We'll be
monitoring him very closely. That's all I
can say at this time.

LIGHTS UP ON VICE PRESIDENTIAL DEBATE SITE,
DEBATE ALREADY IN PROGRESS. **KAMALA HARRIS** IS
SITTING BEHIND DESK, STAGE RIGHT. VICE
PRESIDENT MIKE PENCE, SAME, STAGE LEFT. BOTH
ARE EVIDENTLY TALKING TO THE CAMERAS BUT
NOTHING IS HEARD. FINALLY ...

HARRIS
The President said he wanted "... the people
to remain calm." How calm -

PENCE
I have to weigh in here.

HARRIS
Mister Vice President, I'm speaking.

PENCE
(Shifting, shaking head.) I have to -

HARRIS
(Hand upraised, nodding toward PENCE.) I'm
speaking.

(Both HARRIS and PENCE go static.)

MAN, IN RED LIPSTICK AND A STARK WHITE FACE,
SLIPS IN BEHIND PENCE. HE[SIC] IS IN COSTUME
WITH STIFF HAIRS, WINGS, AND SIX LEGS, IN
MANNER AND FORM PROJECTING A COMMON
HOUSEFLY, BUT DISPLAYING THE PROMINENT
BREASTS OF A FEMALE.

MAN
(High pitched voice.) Bzzzt. Bzzzzt. This is
wrong. Something is definitely wrong here.
I'm attracted but don't know why. (Looks
down.) I can't use that. There's no
sustenance there.

(MAN lifts one "wing" to wipe face.)

Such finely done, gray hair. So neat. So
executive. So lush looking but only for
show. Nothing would survive here. Bzzzzzzzt.

MAN
"SITTING ON A SHOCK OF HIS GRAY"
(Normal tone of voice) *Pence again is*
on the TV,
But there's nothing new here to see.
Listening to debate questions be asked,
Hearing the nonsense he's so eager to
pass.

I'm sitting on a shock of his gray,
Hearing the lies tick away.
Sitting on a shock of his gray,
To watch and wait.

In listening to how Pence debates,
I derive little from what he relates.
Relevant to what is at stake,
His points seem so decidedly fake.

So, I'll sit here on a shock of his
gray,
Listening to lies tick away.
Sitting on a shock of his gray,
To watch and wait.

*Pence can't change horses at this late
date.
He's compelled to make reason be third
rate.
But since everything for him is dogma
and cant,
It easy for him to be comfortable with
Trump's slant.*

*That's why perched here as he intones
Makes a chill seep deep in my bones.
So, I won't stay here for that long,
Just enough for me to finish my song.*

*I sit here on a shock of his gray,
Hearing the lies tick away.
Sitting on a shock of his gray,
To watch and wait.*

Bzzzzzzzzt.

Why did I pick this spot? It seemed like the
stuff I usually am attracted to, except that
I see now there's nothing to absorb or to
use for the future. It just is, with no
redeeming benefit. So, why have I come? Why
am I here?

Help me! Help me! Bzzzzzzzzzt!

(MAN/FLY turns and exits.)

BLACKOUT. THE BUZZING PROGRESSES TO REAR OF
HALL, FADING.

LIGHTS UP ON HALLWAY IN SENATE BUILDING.
SENATORS LINDSEY GRAHAM AND MITCH MCCONNELL
AT MICS BEFORE NEWS PEOPLE.

NEWSPERSON

Senator McConnell, four years ago you said, and I'll read your words: "The American people should have a voice in the selection of their next Supreme Court Justice. Therefore, this vacancy should not be filled until we have a new president." Some argue that Justice Barrett's nomination is being acted on very quickly. How is the situation different now?

MCCONNELL

The difference is that there is a Republican in the White House. That's the story. The End.

GRAHAM

Let me add that what you quoted is from early 2016. This is 2020. We have the Senate and we have the White House. What McConnell and I said years ago is out of date and being taken out of context. There's no question but that Judge Barrett will be the next justice appointed to the Supreme Court. Look, we're just doing what should be done. Like in the good old days of segregation. Ha. Ha. Right?... Now don't you people go taking THAT out of context. I'm being sarcastic.

MCCONNELL

Elections have consequences. This is the Conservative's answer to too many years of a court under Liberal domination. This is our chance to chart a different course.

MCCONNELL
"CLEARLY THIS IS OUR SHOT"

Four years ago I made a vow, no SCOTUS vote would I allow.

Look, Obama's term was nearly done.

With only a year left to serve, he
certainly had some nerve
To think he had the right to appoint
one.

If you'll remember when, other Senators
said then,
That what I, Mitch McConnell, decided
made sense.
Well, I've changed my mind; they've
responded in kind.
For this candidate there'll be no past
tense!

So, I say we should confirm.
They say we shouldn't confirm.
Do confirm; don't confirm. Do we do it
or do we not?
We have the power; I don't care the
late hour,
Clearly this is our shot.

A SCOTUS Justice, appointed for life,
sits well above partisan strife.
Thus, a President's final year seemed a
poor time to act.
I know I said so, but that was a long
time ago.
In twenty twenty we've a quite
different set of facts.

The foolish Biden Rule was merely a
then useful tool
For when a Democrat held the high
office.
With Trump in place here, we've no need
to be fair,
We can proceed exactly however it suits
us.

I say we should confirm.
They say we shouldn't confirm.
Do confirm; don't confirm. Do we do it
or do we not?
We have the power; I don't care the
late hour,
Clearly this is our shot.

There's no need to fear that what I
said that one year
Would permanently define my mentation.
My plan is what I focus on. I don't
care if it's thought a con.
My concern is for the party, not for
the nation.

The Dems can talk or can bitch; I
really don't care which.
The Senate and the President are mine.
I'll make sure that the court, hard
Right for years shall comport,
And God's light on my righteous effort
shall shine.

I say we should confirm.
They say we shouldn't confirm.
Do confirm; don't confirm. Do we do it
or do we not?
We have the power; I don't care the
late hour,
Clearly this is our shot.

Yes, I know there's tradition, but do
note in addition
It's my President who sits in the White
House.
It's now, it's today. Old principles
have little sway.
Face it, all the Democrats can do is
grouse!

The Left wants discussion, and sure,
I'll allow a session,
Though, as Graham said, there's really
no need.
This candidate's a lock, and the
Democrats' protests a crock.
Justice Barrett's confirmation will set
a record for speed.

I say we should confirm.
They say we shouldn't confirm.
Do confirm; don't confirm. Do we do it
or do we not?
We have the power, I don't care the
late hour,
Clearly this is our shot.

We could lose in the national race, a statistically plausible case,
But a Joe Biden won't constrain me one bit.
With the Senate in hand, I, McConnell, shall rule the land,
His tenure won't be worth a bucket of spit!

Even if Biden should win, Trump'll be no has been.
Forget that I once invoked principle not person.
I won't be so crass, as to let this chance pass
And not ensure the Court's Right tilt is certain.

So, I say we should confirm.
They say we shouldn't confirm.
Do confirm; don't confirm. Do we do it or do we not?
We have the power, I don't care the late hour,
Clearly this is our shot.

We have the power, I don't care the late hour,
Clearly this is our shot.

LIGHTS BEGIN TO DIM. IN BACKGROUND, REPRESENTATIVE JORDAN AND SENATOR CRUZ APPROACH, EACH WEARING A GAUDY PARTY HAT.

BLACKOUT.

LIGHTS UP ON BUSY STAGE.

STAGE LEFT: TRUMP SUPPORTERS WATCHING
ELECTION RESULTS ON OVERHEAD MONITORS.

STAGE RIGHT: BIDEN SUPPORTERS LIKEWISE.

STAGE REAR WALL: PROJECTION OF CLOCK SHOWING
TIME'S PASSAGE, OLD MOVIE STYLE. ADJACENT IS
PROJECTION OF A DESK CALENDER PAGE SHOWING
"NOVEMBER 3 - TUESDAY."

> (Watchers move about and react ad
> lib, according to words spoken by
> unseen news commentator.)

NEWS COMMENTATOR
Trump appears to have taken Texas. He is
trending quite strongly, in fact, throughout
most of the Central states.... This is going
to take a while. The extent of voter
participation this year is remarkable.

> (Clock hands move faster. Monitor
> screens go dark. Calendar page shows
> November 4.)

NEWS COMMENTATOR
Earlier today, President Trump demanded
that, the deadlines for voting having past,
the count should halt.

> (Calendar shows Nov. 5.)

NEWS COMMENTATOR
"Stay calm," former Vice President Biden
said today in response to the delay in
getting final results. "Democracy can be
messy," he added. President Trump, however,
continues to claim voter fraud without
providing specific evidence.

> (Calendar shows Nov.6, then Nov. 7,
> etc.)

NEWS COMMENTATOR
No decision in Georgia yet, but Biden is
gaining ground. In Pennsylvania, the major
networks, including Fox, have projected that
Biden has won its electoral votes. This
means ... (voice fades)

(Calendar pages flip more rapidly -
Nov. 8, 9,... 17, etc.)

(Vice President BIDEN enters to
address his supporters, who greet him
with applause and cheers.)

BIDEN
Thank you, thank you. A new day is dawning
for America. The delay in starting the
transition to a new administration is
unconscionable but will not impede us. The
road ahead is clear.

BIDEN (WITH SUPPORTERS)
"THE VOTERS HAVE SPOKEN"
(Reggae beat) *The voters have spoken,*
Trump's reign is done.
That he won't concede comes as no
surprise.
He can protest but clearly we have won.
We're going to govern (to govern)
govern without the lies.
My promise is to serve (to serve)
serve each and every one.

Trump's threat to democracy is now of
the past.
You can expect civility in D.C. once
more.
We'll get back to governing fairly at
long last.

We're going to make (to make)
make our economy soar
And are going to rebuild (to rebuild)
rebuild with a far different cast.

Look, America's bright promise is so
rich and so rare.
Here's the thing, it's one that all
should share.
All should share.

The voters have spoken, Trump's reign
is done.
That he won't concede comes as no
surprise.
He can make false claims but clearly we
have won.
We're going to govern (govern) without
the lies.

(Gradual build of cheering.)

He can protest but clearly (clearly) we
have won.
We're going to govern (govern) without
the lies.
And are going to rebuild (to rebuild)
rebuild with a far different cast.
My promise is to serve (to serve)
serve each and every one.
He can make false claims but clearly
(clearly) we have won.

LIGHTS ON BIDEN AND HIS SUPPORTERS FADE.

(TRUMP enters and acknowledges his supporters' acclaim. He shakes his head and grimaces.)

TRUMP

See? They stole the election that I clearly won, just as I said they would. So much fraud. So much, so much. It's hard to believe how much fraud. But I'm not letting America become another Socialist state. I'm going to fight to get the fair and true result that I promised. Because of COVID and the new voting procedures — the disastrous mail-in ballots, for example — this election should have been postponed until after we had a vaccine. We should have called it off.

TRUMP
"CALL THE WHOLE THING OFF"

This election is one I've clearly won.
You can be quite sure of that.
But late ballots and secret counts
Have put the outcome under a cloud.

We'll wait for weeks and still not know
Who really got the most votes.
The election is a total disaster.
Something must be done!

The voting laws this time are different from last time.
Leftists made changes that were clearly out of line.
This time, last time; changes out of line.
We have to call the whole thing off.

The election was rigged; the stealing couldn't be clearer.
Made Miss Liberty a fraud; the Democrats jeer her.
Rigging, stealing; fraud and jeering!
I should call the whole thing off.

They say I can't call the whole thing off,
That voting must run its course.
But once the voting's run its course,
Giuliani will take it to the courts.

I said stop the count; they said all ballots must count.
I said mailed votes don't count; they said those mailed do count.
Count's done, not done; mailed votes aren't real votes!
We must call the whole thing off.

Ballots left my name off; some weren't asked for.
Some ballots were burnt; some thrown in a dumpster.
On purpose, not misprints; shocking, not error.
More reasons to call the whole thing off.

They claim I can't call the whole thing off,
That the counting has days to run.
But once the counting has been done,
Giuliani will take it to the courts.

I say I've won; he says he's won.
I know I've more votes; he says I've
less votes.
I've won, he's won; more votes, less
votes.
What's right is to call the whole thing
off.

My people have the real count; his
touts give a false count.
Real media shows that he's out; fake
media claims that I'm out.
Real count, false count; real news,
fake news.
Better to have called the whole thing
off.

I can still write the whole thing off,
Avoid transfer and have continuation.
I can still prove that I've won.
Giuliani will do it in the courts.

SO, my people have the real count; his
touts gave a false count.
Real media knows that he's out; fake
media claims that I'm out.
Real count, false count; real news,
fake news.

I'll do better calling the whole thing
off.
No transition; instead continuation.
I'll prove that in fact I've won.
Giuliani will do it in the courts.

BLACKOUT.

LIGHTS UP ON EMPTY STAGE. LARGE BANNER ACROSS REAR: "JOE BIDEN, THE 46TH PRESIDENT OF THE UNITED STATES" MC AT MICROPHONE AS STAGE GRADUALLY FILLS WITH MASKED SUPPORTERS.

MC
President-elect Biden has begun the process of transition, as specified in the Constitution. His schedule is very tight but he has agreed to make a brief appearance here this afternoon. (Cheers) Now, when he comes in, you'll greet him warmly. But have your song sheets ready. As soon as I put up my hands, like this (he raises both fists with thumbs up), there'll be a very brief musical phrase and we'll start singing "My Country, 'Tis of Thee."

(Supporters clap and cheer.)

MC
Remember, wait for my signal and the musical intro. Then you –

(TRUMP, in golf togs with club in hand, enters and interrupts.)

TRUMP
Look at you! All wearing those silly face masks. It's a fact, a scientific fact that they don't help against COVID. The FDC and the CDC just made a big story out of it to sway the election. Everyone knows that; everyone sees that. Your Biden didn't win. I did, by millions and millions of votes. We're going to court, probably even the Supreme Court, and we'll prove that. So you've nothing to celebrate. I have. I've had my COVID and I feel better than ever! So much for all that scare talk from Fauci and the other crazies.

(Crowd silently backs off stage. MC
leaves microphone and follows.)

(TRUMP drops a ball at his feet,
takes a practice swing. He looks up
and out.)

TRUMP
Rudy! Where's Rudy?

OFFSTAGE VOICE
He's being interviewed, Mister President. He
has several from your legal team with him.

STAGE LIGHTS BEGIN TO FADE.

TRUMP
That's good. We need all the good media
exposure we can get.

BLACKOUT.

LIGHTS UP ON RUDY GIULIANI IN ARM CHAIR
FACING THREE INTERVIEWERS. HE IS ACCOMPANIED
BY LIFE-SIZED STICK PUPPETS, IN CHAIRS TO
EITHER SIDE: (A) **M.T. GREENE,** OF GEORGIA, A
BLONDE BARBIE CLUB CHELSEA WITH WRINKLED
BROW; (B) **SIDNEY POWELL,** OF DALLAS, STERN-
FACED, WAVING A FLOPPY RUBBER OCTOPUS ON A
STICK (A KRAKEN), HER CHIPMUNK TEETH A
PROMINENT FEATURE; AND (C) **MELISSA CARONE,**
HAIR PILED HIGH ON HER CONTINUALLY ROCKING
HEAD, GLASSES LOW ON NOSE.

GIULIANI
(Responding to prior question) ... Certainly
there's been voter fraud. On a massive
scale.

INTERVIEWER ONE
But haven't election officials stated that
hasn't happened? That voting was not
compromised in any significant way? Are they
lying?

GIULIANI
I'll answer that this way: This is
Washington, D.C., named after our first
great president, the president who was
famous for saying he would never, never tell
a lie. Yet here we are, listening to lie
after lie after lie from a major political
party, the Democrats. Lying is a way of life
for them and the biased media.

INTERVIEWER TWO
What's the truth then?

GIULIANI
The truth is that President Trump did NOT
lose this election. We have several suits
pending, at the state levels, after which
we'll present to the Supreme Court. They
need to hear of these matters.

INTERVIEWER THREE
But haven't most of the cases already been
dismissed?

GIULIANI
Some, but not all.

GREENE PUPPET
They're lying to the American people. In
Georgia, for example, it's pure fraud. Joe
Biden didn't win Georgia. Another recount
will prove that! Georgia is a Red state. We
did not elect Sleepy Joe. He's not going to
be my President!

GREENE PUPPET
"RED THROUGH AND THROUGH"
(A cappella, intensely) *Georgia, oh
sweet Georgia,*
Georgia, Red through and through.
There is no way
That Georgia'd vote for Blue.

Georgia, in my Georgia,
The stated count's not true.
Biden, there is no way
That Georgia'd vote for you.

POWELL PUPPET

Of course not. The only reason he got the count he did was because the voting machines were rigged. It was communist money. The Dominion voting machines were altered by Hugo Chavez to favor Biden and to drop out the Trump votes.

> (She waves the Kraken figure about as she sings.)

POWELL PUPPET
"HANG ON, DONALD"

(A cappella, rousing) *Hang on, Donald.*
Donald, hang on.
Hang on, Donald.
Donald, hang on.

Donald, everyone knows the Democrats
planned to cheat.
And everybody, yes, knew you were
impossible to beat.
Donald, we don't care what the pencil
necks do and say.
You're the one who won this year. It's
clear as day.

So I tell you ...
Hang on, Donald.
Donald, hang on.
Hang on, Donald.
Donald, hang on.

INTERVIEWER TWO
Is that true, Mister Giuliani? Is that your
position, the position of President Trump's
legal team?

GIULIANI
Well, it's true that President Trump won
reelection. But Miz Powell is not a member
of the team at this juncture, although we do
take her allegations seriously. I want to
reiterate —

CARONE PUPPET
(Cutting GIULIANI off) And what about that
Michigan thing? The poll book is off by a
hundred thousand votes. One, two, three, a
hundred. (Moving aback and forth) What did
those guys do? Take it? Do something with
it? Dead people voted. Can you understand
that? Dead people, and illegals!

CARONE PUPPET
"WE WERE CHEATED"
(Briskly syncopated speech)
We were cheated. We were cheated.
Google Gobble. Gooble Gobble.
Votes got tossed. Votes got tossed.
Google Gobble. Gooble Gobble.

It was stolen. It was stolen.
Google Gobble. Gooble Gobble.
We were cheated. We were cheated.
Google Gobble. Gooble Gobble.

INTERVIEWER ONE
(Wry smile, rubbing his chin) I'd like to
get back to you, Mister Giuliani. We've
heard some rather outrageous accusations.
Can you offer any proof?

INTERVIEWER TWO
(To GIULIANI) Yes, it doesn't help clarify
the situation to be putting out wild and
totally unsubstantiated allegations that
merely repeat —

GIULIANI
They're not unsubstantiated. We have proof.

INTERVIEWER THREE
Well, you haven't provided any.

GIULIANI
Shut up, moron. You don't know what you're
talking about! I have proof.

INTERVIEWER THREE
Well, sir, if that's the case, you need to
present it, to the court if nowhere else,
and provide validation.

GIULIANI
Shut up. Shut up. You don't know what you're
talking about! I'm the only one who can do a
proper investigation. I'm a defense
attorney. I decide what's proof!

THE STIFF FIGURE OF GEORGE WASHINGTON ENTERS
FROM STAGE REAR, ACCOMPANIED BY A DRAMATIC
ORCHESTRAL FLOURISH. IT SLOWLY APPROACHES
GIULIANI, ITS LOWER PORTIONS OBSCURED BY
CLOUDS, ALA GILBERT STUART.

THE REMAINDER PROCEEDS PER THE CONFRONTATION
OF THE COMMENDATORE WITH MOZART'S DON
GIOVANNI.

WASHINGTON
Giuliani, I am displeased with you.
You evoke me, yet speak what is not
true.

GIULIANI

Be careful when you speak such slander.
My words are backed by proven fact.

(GIULIANI points to puppet figures.)

Here are my witnesses, they will attest
To the truth, of everything I say.

PUPPETS

Oh, Rudy, oh, Rudy.
Don't argue with him!

GIULIANI

I will argue.

WASHINGTON

You do argue, but not for truth, rather
to subvert truth.
You use your intelligence in aid of a
deceiver.
Fools speak from ignorance and thus can
be excused.
You are far worse than such a one, than
such a fool!

GIULIANI

I do my job. I do as asked. What do you
want?

PUPPETS

We see where this is going.
Rudy can't win.

WASHINGTON

Sophist! Stop this! That argument is
far too old and weak.

GIULIANI
*Speak then. Tell me what it is you ask
of me.*

WASHINGTON
*Admit you know you are as guilty as the
one whom you serve.*

PUPPETS
Don't answer! It's a trick.

GIULIANI
*Tell me, then, tell me what would you
have me do.*

PUPPETS
No, Rudy. Say nothing!

WASHINGTON
*You are schooled in administration and
in the law.
You once led New York with skill and
reason.
So, I ask of you, please tell me,
Why do you bend your skills to poison
both of these?*

PUPPETS
*Don't answer! Can't you see it's a
trick?*

GIULIANI
*Not so! I don't bend to serve.
I am of my own mind.*

WASHINGTON
Be honest!

GIULIANI

I am being honest.

WASHINGTON

Truthfully honest?

PUPPETS

Say yes! Say yes!

GIULIANI

What I do, I do for sake of party.
No, no, I am not ashamed.

WASHINGTON

Then give me your hand to affirm that.

GIULIANI

Here. Here it is.
Owww!

WASHINGTON

What is it?

GIULIANI

Must you squeeze so hard!?!

WASHINGTON

Time is short. Admit it is Trump
To whom you are loyal, not to truth.

GIULIANI

No, No. I'm a lawyer.
I am loyal to my client.

WASHINGTON

Admit, your client lies.

GIULIANI

No. You're an ideal. He and I are real.

WASHINGTON

Admit it.

GIULIANI

No.

WASHINGTON

Admit it! Admit it!

GIULIANI

No! No!

> (PPE draped **SPECTERS** appear and
> surround GIULIANI.)

WASHINGTON

Then this shall be the end for you.

GIULIANI

What are you doing to me?
I feel weak, I feel hot.
Are you making me ill? Is it COVID?
Have you given me COVID?

SPECTERS

Breathless nights and days will reward
you.
You shall linger and you shall die.

GIULIANI

I am afraid of it. I'm too old to
survive it.
What if I have made a mistake?
What if, to please a potent present,
I have been servile, dishonorable?

SPECTERS

Yet, in the hands of those you've maligned,
You'll receive better than you have given.

GIULIANI

(Being dragged off)
What if, with honor and loyalty cast aside,
I am remembered as dishonorable, servile?
Could the old fool be right?
I would be lost!
Have I made a mistake? Many?
Ahhhh, forever lost!

PUPPETS

His words will serve to mock him.
His deeds will serve to shadow him.
His lies will serve to define him.
We needed such as he. We needed him.
What will become of us?

Ahhhhhh!

His words will serve to mock him.
His deeds will serve to shadow him.
His lies will serve to define him.
We needed such as he. We needed him.
Ahhh, what will become of us?

INTERVIEWER TWO

(Aside) Who's he talking to??? Do you see anyone? The ghost of that sex offender slash "poll watcher" he showed up with in Philly?

INTERVIEWER THREE

I don't see anyone. There are those three
puppets that he was playing with, but ...

INTERVIEWER TWO

He's having some kind of meltdown.

INTERVIEWER THREE

Could he be talking to them? The puppets?
Hallucinating? If so ... Wow. Rather sad,
actually. These past few years it's been
hard to recognize him as the guy who once
ran New York, the greatest city. "Mayor of
World" is what they called him. And a
powerful prosecutor. Now he's ... I don't
know ... doing a grotesque Sesame Street???

(Pause.)

INTERVIEWER ONE

Well, we need to wrap this up.

BLACKOUT.

AT LIGHTS UP, STAGE IS EMPTY EXCEPT FOR
MICROPHONE CENTER FRONT. PRESIDENT-ELECT JOE
BIDEN AND DR. JILL BIDEN, BOTH MASKED, ENTER
AND APPROACH MIC. JOE BIDEN RELEASES HIS
WIFE'S HAND AND REMOVES HIS MASK, TOUCHES
THE MIC.

BIDEN

Friends, Twenty twenty has been a hard year.
The COVID pandemic has made it a year of
tragedy and sacrifice for many Americans.
It's also been a year of partisan political
struggle. But we can look forward with hope.
A vaccine, several, in fact, are now being
distributed that will bring that scourge to
an end. That will not happen overnight. But
it's coming. Also, the nation's Electoral
College has spoken and affirmed that I will
be your next President. The outgoing
President has not seen fit to acknowledge

this fact and is making the Constitutionally mandated transition more difficult. Nevertheless, I'm putting together my administrative team, which, I promise you, shall work with me for ALL Americans, regardless of party affiliation.

To you, my friends, I say there will be a new dawn in America and a new era of opportunity for all, of fairness for all, of concern for all. And to you, Mister President, I say, stand down, follow the dictates of good sense and the Constitution.

BIDEN
"HIT THE ROAD, MAN"

(Sternly) *Hit the road, man. Stick with the plan.*
The plan, the plan, the plan, the plan.
Hit the road, man, don't mess up the plan.
That's what I say!
Hit the road, man. Stick with the plan.
The plan, the plan, the plan, the plan.
Hit the road, man, don't mess up America's plan.

Oh, Donald, Oh, Donald, give up your vain fight.
Just because your base cheers doesn't make it right.
Our Constitution has it so.
It's time to pack up your things and go!
> (CAST gradually filters in and takes up the chorus, facing BIDEN.)

Hit the road, clown. It's time to stand down.
Stand down, stand down, stand down, stand down.
Hit the road, clown, don't mess up the plan.
Listen when we say,
Hit the road, man. It's time to stand down.
Stand down, stand down, stand down, stand down.
Hit the road, man, don't mess up America's plan.

Your straw hair and orange face made you much like a clown
Don't make things worse by putting Democracy down.
Our Constitution has it so.
It's time to pack up your things and go!

Hit the road, clown. Stick with the plan.
The plan, the plan, the plan, the plan.
Hit the road, clown, don't gum up the plan.
The time has come!
Hit the road, clown. Stick with the plan.
The plan, the plan, the plan, the plan.
Hit the road, clown, don't gum up America's plan.

The voting is over and it's clear that
I've won.
Your complaining and inciting are
helping no one.
The electoral votes are solid and mine,
Your fomenting of anger won't change a
line.
Our Constitution has it so.
It's time to pack up your things and
go!

So, hit the road, Don. Honor the plan.
The plan, the plan, the plan, the plan.
Hit the road, Don, and don't mess up
the plan.
It's what we say!
Hit the road, man. Honor America's
plan.
The plan, the plan, the plan, the plan.
Hit the road, man, don't mess up
America's plan.

(Music continues as all slowly turn
to face audience.)

MAN, NO LONGER IN WHITE FACE, ENTERS TO
STAND STAGE RIGHT. HE IS HIGHLIGHTED AS
STAGE LIGHTS DIM.

MAN
It's late December of twenty twenty. It's
the end of a story but not the end of THE
story. Twenty twenty-one will come with its
own problems, you can be sure., with which
we'll have to deal. We may even have to wait
until 2024 to gauge the viability of
American democracy as we know it. COVID will

be defeated. Yes, I promise you that. But that's not the only disease infecting our country.

Our doctors and scientists have created vaccines to treat COVID-19. Theirs is an early and most welcome Christmas gift. And they, not any political figure or political party deserve the credit. Perhaps that model of intense effort and cooperation can be used to conquer other dread diseases. But, so far, I'm afraid, there's no vaccine against extremism. Nor can we hope for one. Fear and anger, envy and resentment will always be with us. While ever ready to expand to epidemic proportions, they can be overcome. We can be proud that we did so in twenty twenty.

However, my friends, as these past several years have shown, there are modern means to exacerbate them and many who are willing to do so. We must continue the fight against extremism. We must deny it the fuel for growth, ensure that it does not poison the promise and prospects of this great nation.

That we came so close to losing that battle must come as an awakening. Join us in singing "My Country 'Tis of Thee," the song that reminds each of us of what we, individually and together, stand to lose and why we must be diligent and strong.

> (MAN points upstage, where the words are projected on back wall. All sing.

ALL
"MY COUNTRY, 'TIS OF THEE"
My country, 'tis of Thee,
Sweet Land of Liberty
Of thee I sing;

Land where my fathers died,
Land of the pilgrims' pride,
From every mountain side
Let Freedom ring.

My native country, thee,
Land of the noble free,
Thy name I love;
I love thy rocks and rills,
Thy woods and templed hills,
My heart with rapture thrills
Like that above.

HOUSE LIGHTS UP

(CAST approaches stage apron as they
sing, some linking arms.)

Let music swell the breeze,
And ring from all the trees
Sweet Freedom's song;
Let mortal tongues awake;
Let all that breathe partake;
Let rocks their silence break,
The sound prolong.

Our fathers' God to Thee,
Author of Liberty,
To thee we sing,
Long may our land be bright
With Freedom's holy light ...

DISRUPTIVE SHOUTS OF "MAGA, MAKE AMERICA
GREAT AGAIN, MAGA" COME FROM REAR OF
AUDIENCE. A GROUP OF TRUMP SUPPORTERS IN RED
VESTS AND MAGA HATS COMES UP THE AISLE,

TRUMP

We own that song as much as you. I'm going
to make America great again! It's what they
wanted. I'm not here by accident.

> (At foot of stage, TRUMP turns to
> face audience.)

I came from you. Remember? You voted for me
in 2016, and in 2020 more than seventy
million of you voted for me to stay.

SENATORS TED CRUZ AND HAWLEY EMERGE FROM
TRUMP'S ENTOURAGE TO STAND CLOSE BEHIND HIM.
BOTH ARE CARTOONISH, DRESSED IN GARISH
YELLOW AND BLACK CHECKED SUITS AND WEARING
OUTSIZED CLOWN SHOES.

CRUZ AND HAWLEY
"STICK TO HIM"

*We will stick to him, stick to him,
stick to him.*
*Whether or not we believe him, believe
him, believe him.*

We won't question him,
Whatever he may say,
Whatever he declaims or tweets out.
There's nothing we can't justify.
He's in command of the G.O.P.

> (CRUZ puts on a red clown nose. TRUMP
> examines him quizzically.)

We need him, we need him, we need him.
His tweets will reach so many, so many,
so many.

His core will stay fiercely loyal, so
loyal, so loyal.
It's support that we will draw on, will
draw on, will draw on.

We have ambitious plans.
Obviously we aim to rise far above.
In him we have that potent ally,
So we give him that abundant love.
His base is a treasure trove.

(To TRUMP) In you we have that potent
ally,
So we give you our abundant love.
Your base is a treasure trove.

We will stick to him, stick to him,
stick to him.
Whether or not we believe him, believe
him, believe him.

We won't question him,
Whatever he may say,
Whatever he declaims or tweets out.
There's nothing we can't justify.
He's in command of the G.O.P.

      (CRUZ shifts closer to TRUMP,
      endeavoring to catch his eye.)

TRUMP
(To CRUZ, curtly) That'll do, Tod.

CRUZ
It's "Ted," not "Tod."

                            TRUMP
Tod, Ted, whatever. I don't care. That'll
do, Cruz.

          (HAWLEY looks downcast. He starts to
          speak but is interrupted.)

                            TRUMP
(To MAN) See? What you call extremism is
just people loving me and disagreeing with
you. Isn't that right? Everyone knows that.
Instead of whining, you should be thanking
me for the early Christmas present of a
COVID vaccine. Be like me: Make the best of
the good news and use the bad for blaming.

(To audience) The trick is to turn the bad
news around, change it or simply ignore it.
That works, as you well know. Everybody
knows that. I long ago learned that you
actually prefer that. The best leaders do
that. And I'm one of the best this country's
had.

So, go ahead and sing with Joe, if you want
to. Sing while you have that chance, while
you have your four years. But four years is
a short time. My people and I have plenty of
time and we're not going anywhere.

                            TRUMP
                  "I DON'T NEED TO HEAR"
     (Vigorously up-tempo country)
     *I don't need to hear that people are
     dying from COVID.*
     *I've no need to weep aloud as the death
     toll mounts.*
     *I don't need to hear I could've done it
     better than I did.*
     *That we have a vaccine now is all that
     counts.*

                         - 188 -

I don't need to hear that Russia's an
evil hacker.
The Democrats have been preaching that
for far too long.
Putin is my friend. He'd never stab us
in the back here.
He's told me so and there's nothing to
prove him wrong.

Barr wouldn't say that.
He'll soon be gone now.
He should've been more loyal.
Still, he's better than any who'll
follow.

Go ahead and sing your song.
Celebrate America your own way.
Don't expect to see me change.
My hard Right vision is here to stay.

I don't need to hear who created that
COVID vaccine.
It doesn't matter. It was done because
of me.
Whatever the coming year brings upon
the world scene,
You can count on my Conservative
legacy.

I don't need to hear Dems whine that
mine are hollow slogans.
Image is the key and I've made sure
that my base loves me.

If doing wrong does me right I can
always promise pardons,
And keep supporters close and firm in a
web of complicity.

2020 has been a hard year.
What's coming next is hard to tell.
But, as was proven throughout my term,
Misery will give me something to sell.

Fine, do sing your song.
Celebrate America your fake way.
Don't expect to see me change.
My hard Right vision is here to stay.

    (BIDEN and his supporters begin to
    drift offstage.)

I don't want to hear my first election
was accidental.
I'm here because of you and here I'll
stay.
I don't care if Biden has a nasty Blue
bent.
My Red spirit won't be going away.

I have no plans to attend his
inauguration.
What they'll put on is not my kind of
show.
He'll make promises that will certainly
ruin the nation.
So if G.O.P. leaders were smart they
wouldn't go.

The election was stolen.
There was fraud at the polls.
SCOTUS wouldn't help me.
Even with proof in the totals.

Yes, do sing your song.
Celebrate America your own way.
But don't expect the world to change.
My hard Right vision is here to stay.

You need to know that I'm planning on a
comeback.
With nearly half on my side you can be
sure of that.
You'll see me revive our Conservative
core track.
And you can count on me wearing my
bright Red hat.

If I'm not the one leading the
reactionary campaigns,
Whoever it is will be wearing my Red
MAGA hat.
If not me, then it's someone like me
who will take the reins,
With nearly half on our side, you can
be sure of that.

Yes, do sing your song.
Celebrate America your own way.
But don't expect the world will change.
My hard Right vision is here to stay.

*No, don't expect the core of the world
will change.
The hard Right vision I brought out is
here to stay.
No, don't expect the core of the world
will change.
The hard Right vision I brought out is
here to stay.*

LIGHTING ISOLATES A DEFIANT TRUMP. HIS
SUPPORTERS GATHER CLOSE ABOUT HIM

*No, don't expect the core of the world
will change.
The hard Right vision I brought out is
here to stay.
No, don't expect the core of the world
will change.
The hard Right vision I brought out is
here to stay.*

*Yes, do sing your song.
Celebrate America your own way.
But don't expect the world will change.
My hard Right vision is here to stay.*

*Yes, do sing your song.
Celebrate America your own way.
But don't expect the world will change.
My hard Right vision is here to stay.*

SLOW FADE OF MUSIC AND STAGE LIGHTS.

BLACKOUT.

END

OF 2020

ADDENDUM
January 11, 2021

The focus of *2020 Hindsight, Trump* is the flow of events during 2020. That year began with the impeachment trial of a sitting president, was made further notable by a pandemic, and finally culminated in a nationwide vote that was marred by prior- and post-election seditious attacks upon it and even upon the procedures with which it was carried out. I wrote *2020 Hindsight, Trump* as the events transpired, to better capture the reality of the participants. As profoundly distressing but historically familiar as were some of the political and social upheavals of that year, as clear as were the lessons being taught and the dire forebodings that bore consideration, it was predetermined that the play would not present anything of 2021. Whatever the outcome of November's election, its consequences for 2021 and beyond will comprise another tale.

However, on January 6, 2021 — a date that will live in infamy — the halls of the Congress of the United States were deliberately and viciously attacked by hordes of insurrectionists incited by the then President, Donald John Trump. Instead of moving forward with the transition to a new administration, he had persisted in his deranged tirades against the election's result, continued to declaim unproven, and in fact easily refutable charges that he won "in a landslide," that the "election was stolen" from him. Having taken an oath to defend the Constitution, he nonetheless encouraged rioters to assemble in our national capital city, requested that they march upon the Capitol building, and "... be strong" in a violent attack upon the core of our democracy. His lawyer and close advisor, Rudy Giuliani, addressed those supporters on that same day, declaiming, "Let's have a trial by combat." His son, Donald Trump, Jr. warned, "We are coming for you."

These quotes are not my hyperbole but rather the speakers' actual words, in context. That the dialogue and lyrics of Act Three, in particular, of *2020 Hindsight, Trump,* written in December of that year, so clearly anticipate the events of early 2021 is testimony not to insight but to the clear manner in which the intentions of those depicted had been signaled months, even years before. Shame on those in the GOP who refused to acknowledge that obvious fact.

Whatever the eventual laying on and disposition of charges against Trump — sedition, incitement to violence, slander, and/or the abject and pitiable stupidity of a sick mind — and whatever the form of his eventual removal — impeachment, resignation, disqualification under Article 25, slinking off — he has damaged America far beyond the stated fears of his political opponents and, at the time of setting them down, the arguably elaborated representations in this play. His vocal and procedural political supporters within the GOP — Cruz, Hawley, Jordan, Graham, to name the most culpable — should be more than ashamed, they deserve condemnation and profound, lasting contempt for their actions during Trump's final months in office and for abetting the unmistakable harm to our democratic institutions that he single-mindedly brought about. And as to his staff and aides, who reiterated his maliciously fake charges in the final weeks of 2020 and were complicit in his persistent criminality against America and its Constitution, they, too, deserve swift and lasting condemnation. Chief among these, of course, is Rudy Giuliani. **The warning is clear:** They are but the shadows of a future yet to come. Beware Trump's disciples, those far younger and more agile, who are even now are organizing to fulfill his vision of an autocratic America dominated by dogma, deceit, and intimidation, who mock and cast aside facts, reason, and compromise.

This musical play, *2020 Hindsight, Trump* is the fourth and final part the "Trump Cycle." Its precursors are: the novel *To Be, and Not To Be*; the allegory *Nuts;* and the stage play/musical ***! TRUMP! ***. The thematic tetrad has its origins in the futuristic *To Be,* preliminarily published in 2013, through which I attempted to convey the very real possibility of a renewal of autocratic Fascism, its insertion here, and its danger to American democracy. Recent events have taken those fears into the realm of chilling, confirmatory reality.

RML

Made in the USA
Middletown, DE
20 February 2021